THE MATERIALIST CONCEPTION
OF HISTORY

THE MATERIALIST CONCEPTION OF HISTORY

A CRITICAL ANALYSIS

BY

KARL FEDERN

AUTHOR OF

" DANTE AND HIS TIME ", " RICHELIEU ", " MAZARIN ", ETC.

GREENWOOD PRESS, PUBLISHERS
WESTPORT, CONNECTICUT

Originally published in 1939
by Macmillan and Company, Ltd., London

First Greenwood Reprinting 1971

Library of Congress Catalogue Card Number 75-114523

SBN 8371-4789-1

Printed in the United States of America

Le philosophe, comme le navigateur, doit se méfier des courants ; et, plus ils sont violents, plus il doit s'en écarter.

GABRIEL TARDE

CONTENTS

CHAPTER VIII

PREFACE

OF the numerous theories which, in the course of history, have been put forth to explain the development of mankind and the causal links between the single historical events and changes, one, in our time, has had a greater success than all others. This is the theory enunciated by Karl Marx and Friedrich Engels, accepted and further developed by their followers. It is commonly called the materialist theory of history or historical materialism, though the name is misleading, and Engels himself proposed to call it the economic theory of history.

According to this theory, economic phenomena and, in the first place, economic production are assumed to be fundamental, while all that we call culture, religion, politics, social and intellectual life are considered as secondary phenomena, determined by the mode of production and the social conditions which are its immediate consequence. It is not the only theory in which the phenomena of man's life and history are traced back to a single group, declared to be basic. Gobineau and his adherents consider race and racial qualities to be the fundamental agency in history; they believe that the destinies of nations as well as those of individuals are in the last resort determined by racial disposition and by the mixture of races, and they are of opinion that this is the only way to understand and to explain the history of man. Hippolyte Taine believed that all individual character and all historical events are a compound of race, environment and the immediate momentary situation.

Now, it is not to be supposed that either of these authors could have been of the naïve opinion that causation ceases with those phenomena which they believed to be basic, and that economics, race, environment or the present situation are self-created and inexplicable. They thought, perhaps, that any further investigation would lead them too far, that they would have to deal with elements which cannot be explained historically. Race, for instance, one might say, is a fact which no longer belongs to the sphere of history but to that of natural science. Just as nobody thinks of tracing back historical events to the anatomy and physiology of the acting persons, or to the chemical and physical conditions of their environment, just as little, these authors might say, does it seem necessary to investigate the elements constituting those primary phenomena. We do not think that this argument, which we perhaps wrongly attribute to them, will hold water. It seems much more probable that, enraptured with their discoveries, they did not even for a moment entertain the thought that the causes which produced the " basic " facts ought to be investigated, and if the problem ever presented itself to them, they turned from it and refused to delve into the matter.

Gobineau's theory has, especially in our time, owing to the conclusions which his adherents drew from it, and their political consequences, gained an importance that is out of proportion to its scientific merit. Much greater, however, is undoubtedly the influence which the " economic " theory has had on the political and scientific development of our period. One palpable reason of its success is that economy and economic facts are really of great importance in the life of every individual and hence in history, and that we have become conscious of their importance. Though the number of historians who have adopted the theory is comparatively small, the Labour Parties in almost all countries have made it a part of their doctrine. In Russia, that is, in a country inhabited by more than 150 millions, it has been officially declared to be the sole true theory and nobody is allowed to teach or to write anything that runs counter to it.

There are, however, more reasons to account for its success than the one mentioned above. The theory appears, at first sight, extremely clear and ingenious. Reducing all historical developments to comparatively simple processes, and explaining them by facts which are, so to speak, palpable and very easily stated, it appeals by its simplicity and lucidity. Young people, in particular, are easily converted to it ; they feel as if their eyes had suddenly been opened ; they are surprised not to have found out all this long ago. The economic facts being, as has been said, of extreme importance in life and history, it is easy to group all other phenomena around them so that they seem to flow from them. One need but describe and arrange the facts in a certain manner, and all will appear logical and conclusive. Marxist historians, as a rule, carefully disregard certain causal inter-connections, which exist in reality, but not for them, and limit themselves to the consideration and description of certain groups of facts. This is the easier to do as all historiography necessarily consists in detaching a relatively small number of facts from the infinite tissue of reality and arranging them according to the writer's views. And, of course, each carefully refrains from all inquiry as to how the economic conditions, the mode of production, for instance, have themselves been brought about. To the layman, and even to the historian who does not investigate the course of events most minutely, all will seem clear and plausible.

We shall admit that the importance of economic conditions has long been unduly neglected by historians, and that their over-estimation in our time has not been without its good effects. That historians proceeded to study them and their relation to politics and culture was a great and indubitable step forward ; and though this has been done by students, many of whom were not Marxists, it is to a considerable degree due to the influence of Historical Materialism. It is the exclusiveness with which the theory is held by its adherents that makes it wrong.

Fifty years have passed since I first heard of this theory. I felt at once that it was unconvincing, though I was unable to demonstrate it. The problem has occupied me ever since ; I read a large number of works written by followers of the doctrine and I tried to test it by studying and comparing historical developments and events in the present and in the past.

We are to-day in a much more favourable position to understand these developments than ever before. Not only has historical science made enormous progress ; historical research has accumulated a mass of facts formerly unknown and laid bare a great number of threads leading from one nation or race and from one period to the other ; but we ourselves have seen the most momentous historical changes take place before our very eyes. We have been spectators of events and catastrophes such as not every generation of men has witnessed, and this in a period in which publicity is much greater than ever before and events become rapidly known and their consequences visible.

As a historian I have been in a position to study certain epochs very closely; and only a knowledge that accumulates as many details as possible can make us understand a past period; only by tracing every event as exactly as possible back to the facts which led up to it, are we enabled to grasp some of the causal links which inter-connect them. Moreover, as correspondent of a great newspaper during the War, and afterwards when I was working in the German Foreign Office, I had ample opportunity to observe, so to speak, at their immediate source, the political events of several years.

The more I studied the clearer did I see the deficiencies and errors of the theory and how it impedes and endangers the recognition of historical truth. It is the more dangerous since, like all theories which have become the starting-point and the doctrinal basis of a movement, its propositions have been invested with the character of religious dogmas. Whosoever dares to contest them is regarded as a heretic, an ignoramus, or, at best, as an unconscious tool of capitalism; in countries where Marxism is the official philosophy, he is considered an evil-doer and punished as such. Thus the theory has not only become an obstacle to all true knowledge of history, but a serious danger to the freedom and the future development of science in general.

Not a few authors, of course, have attempted to dispute the materialist conception of history. It cannot, however, be said that they were particularly successful. I am not going to discuss these attempts made by Paul

Barth, Masaryk and others; I believe their method was not the right one. Still less effect had the words of those who rejected the theory without further ado, who declared it to be false, but took no pains to refute it. Such a proceeding is unscientific and unprofitable. Simply to reject a theory which has achieved such importance and is accepted by so many millions, is clearly of no avail. What is needed is a close examination of the entire doctrine in order to find out how much truth it contains, and how far it is untenable.

In the ensuing study I shall try to do this. I am going to start from what is called the " classical formulation " of the materialist conception of history, the propositions put forward by Karl Marx in 1859. While considering each of these propositions, we shall discuss what other adherents of the theory have written on the subject, and test their utterances in the light of history itself. In this way we may hope to find out whether the theory offers any real explanation of our history or not.

The tendency of this study is necessarily critical and negative. Such a tendency is often required in the search for truth; it is indispensable to clear away falsehood before the truth can be discovered, and the more luxuriant its growth has been, the deeper truth has become hidden and buried beneath it, the greater the need to destroy it.

I shall, however, in order not to appear purely negative, in a concluding chapter indicate, in large outlines, the real inter-connections and causal links in history.

K. F.

EDGWARE FEB., 1939.

CHAPTER I

MARX'S THEORY OF HISTORY

IN the Introduction to the *Criticism of Political Economy*, by Karl Marx, we find the following propositions : [1]

(1) In the course of social economic production men enter into certain relations, and certain conditions are formed by them, of necessity and independently of their will. These conditions of production correspond to a certain stage of development of the material forces of production.

(2) Conditions of production, taken as a whole, constitute the economic structure of society — this is the material basis on which a superstructure of laws and political institutions is raised and to which certain forms of political consciousness correspond.

(3) The political and intellectual life of a society is determined by the mode of production, as necessitated by the wants of material life.

(4) It is not men's consciousness that determines the forms of existence, but, on the contrary, the social forms of life that determine the consciousness.

(5) Arrived at a certain stage of their development,

[1] *Kritik der Politischen Oekonomie* (5th ed., Stuttgart, 1919), p. lix. The paragraphs as well as the numbers are the author's. As no translation can be absolutely and literally correct, readers will find the German original text in Appendix I.

the material forces of production come into conflict with the existing conditions of production, or — this is but a juristic form of expressing the same fact — with the system of property under which they displayed their activity.

(6) From forms of the development of the forces of production, the conditions of production now turn into fetters of these forces.

(7) Then a period of social revolution sets in.

(8) Owing to the alteration of the economic basis, the whole immense superstructure is, gradually or suddenly, subverted.

(9) In order to understand such a revolution, it is necessary to distinguish between the changes in the conditions of economic production which are a material fact and can be observed and determined with the precision of natural science, on one hand, and on the other, the legal, political, religious, artistic and philosophic — in short, ideological forms in which men become conscious of this conflict and fight it out.

(10) As little as an individual can be judged from the opinion he has of himself, just as little can a revolution be judged from men's consciousness of it. On the contrary, this consciousness is to be explained by the conditions of their material life, by the conflict between the social forces of production and the conditions of production.

(11) No form of society can perish before all the forces of production which it is large enough to contain, are developed, and at no time will outworn conditions be replaced by new higher conditions as long as the material necessities for their existence have not been hatched in the womb of the old society itself.

(12) Mankind never sets itself a problem that it

cannot solve. On close examination it will always be found that no social problem ever arises unless the material conditions which make its solution possible, are either already in existence or at least developing.

(13) In bold outline, one may distinguish between Asiatic, Antique, Feudal and Modern Capitalist [1] forms of production, as being the progressive economic forms of society.

(14) The present Capitalist conditions of production are the last antagonistic form of society; though not in the sense of individual antagonism : the antagonism arises from the social conditions of individuals. The productive forces, however, that are developing under the present system, are at the same time creating the material conditions which will make the solution of this antagonism possible.

(15) This social system represents therefore the closing period of the prehistoric era of human society.

We may look upon these propositions, which have become famous, as the basis of Historical Materialism. They were written in London in the year 1859. Marx says, however, that as early as 1841, when writing a criticism of Hegel's *Philosophy of the Law*, he had become aware of the truth that " constitutions and laws, and the whole organisation of society, cannot be explained by the so-called development of human intellect, but are rooted in the forms of material life ". Eighteen years had to pass before he set about fully developing his ideas. The propositions are couched in the somewhat heavy and obscure philosophical language of the time, though their meaning is quite discernible. They are followed by a number of short sentences jotted down

---

[1] Marx says " bourgeois ".

incoherently, headings, etc.; the whole a kind of draft of what was destined to complete and to illustrate Marx's thought. The *Introduction to the Criticism of Political Economy* remained unfinished, a fragment. Marx never found the necessary time to write a complete work in which to expound his Theory of History; he only sowed the seed from which a new philosophy of history was to germinate. In his other writings, as, for instance, in *Hired Labour and Capital* and in *Capital* itself, we find some similar utterances; in his historical writings like *The 18th Brumaire* and *Class Struggle in France* we may see illustrations of his opinions on history, but nothing important is added to the theory. Only in a posthumous work by Marx and Engels, *German Ideology*, which was not published until 1933, do we find, though interspersed with diffuse polemics against several philosophic writers of the period, some interesting pages on the subject. And in various writings of Friedrich Engels, as well as in his correspondence, there are numerous remarks to be found which may be regarded as comments on the theory.

Marx offered no proofs for his theses; he was satisfied with enunciating them. We shall, however, have to examine not only the theses but also the proofs which other writers have since tried to furnish.

There can be no doubt that the essential point, the main issue of the theory, is contained in the second proposition: " Conditions of production, taken as a whole, constitute the economic structure of society; this is the material basis on which a superstructure of laws and political institutions is raised and to which certain forms of political consciousness correspond ".

The words " legal and political superstructure "

comprise constitutions, laws and jurisdiction, administration, political parties, in fact, the whole political
structure as well as the political life of a given society.
The words " forms of consciousness " comprise religion,
morals, art, science, poetry, opinions, that is, the whole
intellectual life of a given epoch.

In the propositions 5-10, Marx, after adding a short
comment, proceeds to explain the great social revolutions :
changes in the economic structure of society lead to
changes in the political superstructure and in the forms
of consciousness.

Yet, as preliminary to all this, Marx informs us in the
first proposition of two facts, namely, that the conditions
of production which form the economic structure of
society, are " necessary and independent of human will ",
and that they correspond to a certain development of
the productive forces.

One might object to the wording of the proposition
that the term " necessary " is meaningless, and " independent of human will " ambiguous.   To a determinist
all events are effects of causes and, as such, necessary.
The words " independent of human will " either mean
the same thing as " necessary ", or Marx — though this
can hardly be assumed — used the words in their everyday sense, without any reference to the question of free
will or necessity, in order to distinguish between men's
voluntary acts and those facts which are independent of
their will like the soil, the climate, the racial qualities.
Supposing this to be the purport, the sentence would be
false, the conditions of production being undoubtedly
determined in the main by voluntary acts, whether
human will and those acts be, from a philosophical
standpoint, considered as free or not.

We do not, however, assume that this was Marx's meaning. His meaning was undoubtedly that there is a certain compulsion in the conditions of production and that men are driven by necessity to create them. The manufacturer cannot help producing, rationalising, forming trusts ; agriculture is, in a given period, necessarily extensive or intensive ; workmen and capitalists are compelled to make certain agreements. Men's will or their wishes, their hopes and anxieties, have no great influence on all this. Marx probably wished to call his readers' attention to the fact that economic conditions do not depend on what individuals like or dislike, this being but an illusion, that there is a law in them over which men's will is unable to prevail. Knowing that only few people are aware of this, he wanted his readers to discard this illusion and grasp the inherent necessity. Nevertheless, his mode of expression remains inexact and misleading.

Marx leaves no doubt as to the nature of this necessity. He proceeds at once to explain why the conditions of production are inevitably and of necessity such as they are ; they correspond to a certain stage of development of productive forces. That is to say, the conditions of production are determined by the productive forces.

The development of the productive forces is indeed — according to this theory — the *causa causans* in history. The fate and development of mankind are determined by them.

We shall, therefore, have first to examine the truth of this proposition.

CHAPTER II

THE PRODUCTIVE FORCES

WHAT are productive forces ? How do they come into existence and how do they develop ? Are they really the last, or rather the first cause, the primary agency in the economic development of mankind and therewith, according to Historical Materialism, of all history ?

Productive forces are the forces employed in economic production by man, the fertile qualities of the soil, the special properties of metals, the mechanical and chemical forces of nature, solar heat, steam power, electricity, as well as the forces of animals and of man himself.[1]

[1] The term " productive force " seems to have been used for the first time by François Dupin in his work *Situation progressive des forces productives de la France*, published in 1827. It was the German economist, Friedrich List, who introduced it into the terminology of economic science. Cf. Charles Gide and Charles Rist, *Histoire des doctrines économiques* (5th ed., Paris, 1926), p. 235 n. Like many similar terms, it gives only an approximate idea of what is meant by it. The question arises whether the intellectual forces of man belong to the productive forces or not. We do not see how they can well be excluded, considering that they are the sole forces which play an active part in the process of economic production. Yet, for this very reason, their mode of operation being different from that of all other forces, it would be difficult to include them in the same category. Marx and his followers do not seem to have paid much attention to this important question. Marx certainly did not include them among the productive forces mentioned in his theses, for in this case he would have had to change the latter entirely, and the whole theory would have crumbled. He and his adherents relegate all intellectual activities to the " ideological superstructure ".

7

Now, all these productive powers, heat, fertility, water and steam power, all the manifold forces of nature, upon the combination of which economic production depends, are always there; they have existed from time immemorial. It was only necessary to discover them and to find out in what manner they could be put to use.

Magnetism, for instance, and electricity, which play such a conspicuous part in modern economic production, did always exist; but no intelligent human being had discovered them and found out how they might be employed for man's use. There are, no doubt, many undiscovered forces and phenomena in nature which might be of unsuspected value to human economics, waiting to be discovered by man.

Discovering a new productive force, as well as finding out a method of applying it, are mental acts. If this were not the case, if there were no need of intelligence to discover and employ the forces of nature, the animals would discover and employ them also, and the inferior races would develop a civilisation as quickly as the higher do. Probably no one would contend that the discovery and the use of productive forces, from the construction of primitive tools, the domestication of animals, the beginning of agriculture, up to the use of steam and electricity, have been unconscious acts and were not brought about by what we call mind, imagination, reasoning and will, in short, the intellectual activities of man. People may not always be conscious of the importance and of the consequences of their discoveries, but every discovery, the most primitive contrivance as well as the most surprising invention, was made by the imaginative and reasoning forces of the human mind. If these forces were lacking, men would live and act like

8

animals ; the productive forces of nature would remain undiscovered, and there would be neither development nor civilisation. Discoveries and inventions may be necessary, which is to say that they are in no wise exempt from the inter-dependency of cause and effect, but they are due to man's intellect.

We shall have to examine their causation as well as their consequences in order to understand their part in the development of mankind. Before doing this, how-ever, we have to consider an objection which might be raised at this point. Men, one might say, had natural wants ; they stood in need of food, shelter, clothing, etc. Chance made a savage in such need break a bough from a tree, lift a sharp-edged stone from the earth, and make use of them ; by pure chance another savage found the art of kindling a fire ; by chance he tamed the first animal, just as chance would that, in later ages, a civilised man observed and was struck by the effect of steam-power. The discovery once made, the development of the productive force and of the different ways in which it could be used, followed quite naturally. To this we should once more reply, for the moment, that if chance did suffice for the discovery, the animals would discover the forces of nature and construct tools and machinery just as men do : chances are the same for them, only the gift of constructive thought is lacking.

We shall show in another place that the words " chance " and " necessity " are meaningless in history, because either all events are necessary, that is to say, the inevitable consequence of sufficient causes, or none. It is impossible that there should be some necessary events and others that are not necessary ; such an idea is not even thinkable.

9

But, leaving this philosophical discussion and using everyday language, we shall, from a purely human standpoint, call it chance when a savage discovers for the first time a sharp-edged stone that can be used as a knife, or when a civilised man observes that steam lifts the lid of the teapot. Yet, even when looked at from this point of view, it is only the experience that was due to chance, whereas it was due to the person's particular bent or quality of mind that the fact struck him as peculiar and that he drew important conclusions from it. Such chances will occur over and over again for the simple reason that the productive forces are always there, but a sufficiently intelligent being had to come who became aware of the possibility of using the force. Millions of boughs grew on the trees or were lying on the ground, capable of serving as levers or palisades, there were plenty of sharp stones that might be used as knives or axes ; steam lifted the teapot's lid a hundred thousand times ; yet not until a sufficiently intelligent savage decided to make use of the bough or the stone, and not until a gifted man saw that the steam which lifted the teapot's lid, might serve for much greater purposes, was the discovery possible.

It is true that the possibilities of discovery are not always the same ; true that sometimes a productive force is discovered, but is not put to use ; its application to economic purposes would not be possible. When, in the thirteenth century, Roger Bacon in his letter to Master William of Paris " On the secrets of nature and the futility of magic ", predicted steamships, railways, aeroplanes and high explosives, men were much too backward and ignorant to understand him, and they locked him up. When, long before Roger Bacon, Heron of

Alexandria and, at a still earlier date, Archimedes discovered the principle of the steam-engine, many people were cultivated enough to understand it, and technical and economic conditions were even such that its application to production should have been possible. Roman capitalists employed thousands of slaves in great industrial establishments, and their engineers knew how to construct and use complicated machinery. It would be hard to say what prevented the application and development of the new force. When it was rediscovered in the seventeenth and eighteenth centuries by Branca, Papin and Watt, the public took great interest in natural science; people were in the habit of hearing of new discoveries and inventions, and were more ready to believe in new theories and try new methods. This, perhaps, may account for the different manner in which the discovery was received in modern times.

All development, however, is slow and proceeds gradually, owing to an inertia inherent in man's nature, which makes him reluctant to change even if the change be to his advantage. All innovations encounter difficulties, and in all eras it is a few imaginative and energetic individuals who take the lead, the others following reluctantly and distrustfully until the new device has been generally accepted and become habitual. At all times some bold person makes a big step in advance while the rest follow hesitatingly and slowly. Another serious check upon innovations in the economic sphere lies in the fact that an invention or discovery, though conducive to general improvement, may mean great losses to some and even to many persons whose income and position, nay, whose very existence, is threatened by its introduction, and who therefore have an interest in opposing and, if possible, preventing it. It is one of the saddest facts that, at least in the present economic order, invested capital is often being reduced in value owing to new inventions and numberless workmen turned out of employment.

From the foregoing we must deduce that the expression " the development of the productive forces ", as used by Marx, is equivocal and misleading in so far as it is human intellect that discovers and develops one productive force after the other.

Marx knew this, of course ; he says in another passage : " Man develops the powers slumbering in nature and subjects the play of her forces to his command ". We may therefore interpret his opinion as follows :

By whatever means productive forces may be discovered and in whatever period they may be put to use, it is a fact that mankind acquires control in the course of history of an ever-growing number of productive forces, beginning with the most primitive, such as the physical forces of men and beasts, water, fire, the fertility of the soil, and finally discovering forces which, like steam and electricity, can only be put to use by means of complicated appliances. With man's increasing command of the productive forces, the conditions of production change. They correspond to the degree of his command of these forces. As long as man controlled only a few primitive productive forces, conditions of production were simple; along with his increasing use of ever-new productive forces, many of which can only be put to use by complicated methods and contrivances, the conditions of production also become differentiated. Then complicated institutions are established, law-books are compiled and intellectual life develops. All this is clearly a mere superstructure erected on the conditions of production, a reflection of these conditions in man's consciousness. We are therefore entitled to say : the development of the conditions of production is proportionate to that of the forces of production, and along with them develops the ideological superstructure. At times and under certain circumstances, this development proceeds accompanied by terrible convulsions and great disturbances. Yet, social conditions as well as intellectual currents and changes may all be traced back to the extension of man's power over the productive forces of the earth.

We shall not deny that this idea has the appeal of a certain simplicity and even grandeur ; it reveals man in his perennial efforts to make the earth and its forces subservient to his own ends ; it shows how, with man's constant endeavour to utilise these forces, ever more complicated social systems arise and ever new thoughts spring up in men's heads.

One may, however, raise the question whether such simplifying generalisations in which the immensity of the real world is condensed into a few short sentences, the countless facts of history into a few words, do convey any real knowledge. A still more important question is whether, in examining the concatenation of events in history, the formation of institutions and opinions, we shall find that the theory holds good.

If Marx, instead of using the term " development of the productive forces ", had spoken of " men's increasing command over the productive forces ", his mode of expression would have been more in conformity with the facts, and his followers would have been spared many mistaken conclusions.

13

In Alfred Braunthal's treatise *Karl Marx as Philosopher of History*,[1] for instance, we find the following passage : " The materialist conception of history does not attempt to explain the development of the productive forces ; this development explains itself ; it is simply the ultimate fact ". Such an astonishing statement would have been impossible if Marx had expressed himself correctly. Yet, misleading as Marx's way of putting it may have been, it is surprising that a man should seriously assume that the inter-dependency of cause and effect has its end in the productive forces, that they are self-created and that it is useless to investigate their origin. The chain of cause and effect may end at a transcendental cause, a divinity that by definition is inscrutable; but it can never stop at a material phenomenon. Braunthal's opinion reminds us of the dialogue between the European and the Indian. On the European's asserting that the earth is poised in space, the Indian says : " That is madness ; the earth reposes on the back of a giant elephant ". " And where does the elephant stand ? " retorts the European. — " On a giant tortoise." " And the tortoise ? " — " That ", is the Indian's reply, " must not be asked. That question is forbidden."

Not deterred by Braunthal's injunction, we dare to affirm that the development of the productive forces has its cause in acts of the human mind. And if it be true that the human mind is frequently driven to such acts by economic necessities and is itself being developed by such necessities and the actions which they inspire, this truth implies a certain inter-connection and inter-dependency between economic necessities, the human mind and production. So much, however, is certain :

[1] Alfred Braunthal, *Karl Marx als Geschichtsphilosoph*, Berlin, 1920.

14

the productive forces play no active part in this process ; they do not determine the course of development any more than the apple which I eat because I am hungry, or the net which I use for fishing, are the causes of these acts.

There is another point which ought to be elucidated. " The conditions of production ", says Marx, " correspond to a certain stage of the development of the productive forces." Now, which moment in this development is decisive ? Is it that of the discovery of the new force, the day on which it is first put to use, or the time when its use has become general ? It cannot well be the discovery, for centuries and even thousands of years may pass before a discovery is applied to production in such a measure as to have any noteworthy influence on society. There can be no doubt that Marx had in mind the time when the use of a new force has become frequent enough to be of a certain importance for economic production at large, for it is only then that it is enabled to play a part in social development. It is therefore necessary to investigate how the use of any new force becomes general or at least extensive. All Marxists will agree that a certain development of the conditions of production must have been attained before a productive force of a perfectly new kind can be introduced. It would be quite impossible, for instance, to use steam-engines in production unless sufficient capital has been accumulated and a sufficient number of trained workmen, or workmen sufficiently intelligent to make the training possible, are to be found. That, however, would be the reverse of what Marx said. It is not the conditions of production which we find depending on the development of the productive forces, but the pro-

ductive forces which are determined by a certain development of the conditions of production. Should we, then,
have to invert Marx's thesis in order to find the truth?
We should indeed find part of the truth, but not the whole
truth.

Marx disciples have tackled the problem, but it does
not look as if they had found a satisfactory solution.
Professor Heinrich Cunow, for instance, in his work
on Marx's political theories, says: "Whenever new
forces are applied in the entire production—owing, for
example, to the discovery of a new force or to a new
technical invention — the mode of production changes,
and along with it the economic relations — that is, the
conditions of production — which are its results".
And in another passage, arguing against Professor
Werner Sombart, he even says, "Technique itself can
do nothing; it must be applied to production", adding
that, in order to do this, there must be qualified workmen
at one's disposal. And he quotes the answer which
Staudinger returned to Sombart at the Congress of
Sociologists in 1910: "Professor Sombart seems to
forget the intellectual element that is in technique".[1]

It is the development of the human mind that determines the development of the productive forces. No
productive force ever discovers itself, none applies itself
to economic production; it is the human mind that
discovers and applies them. Human minds are so
constituted that they will observe the forces at work in
nature. Some minds are qualified to divine or to discover the possibility of using these forces to satisfy
human needs, and some persons endowed with such

[1] Heinrich Cunow, *Die Marxschen Geschichts-, Gesellschafts- und
Staatstheorien* (4th ed., Berlin, 1923), vol. ii. pp. 162, 178.

minds are able to persuade others to do this. Everything must be present in thought before it can be present in action. This fact is so evident and commonplace that it is constantly overlooked and neglected. Yet unless it is constantly borne in mind, neither human life nor human history can be properly understood.

It is human minds that play the active part in social evolution, whereas the productive forces play only a passive part. In the expression " development of the productive forces " the word " development " has an active sense. The productive forces do not develop : they are being developed.[1]

The whole matter takes on a different aspect if we decide to rate the human mind among the productive forces. In that case we should have to do with a productive force taking an active part in economic development, as in all other spheres of human life. This was the prevailing theory in former times when the course of history was regarded as being shaped to a large extent by the human mind and the evolution of mankind as proportioned to the human mind's development. It was this theory which Marx and his followers arose to defeat, and they tilt at it whenever an occasion to do so presents itself. We saw Marx proclaiming " Laws, institutions, opinions, cannot be explained by the development of the human intellect " ; according to his theory, all men's intellectual and political activity is but a reflection, a superstructure of the conditions of production. In the

---

[1] This becomes still clearer when we consider that the use of steam-power and electricity, on which production in our days essentially depends, is due solely to the discoveries made by the powerful brains of great scientists and to a most complicated machinery such as only the subtlest intelligence could invent and construct. As to an objection made to this argument, cf. pp. 91 *sqq.*

course of this study we shall have to examine the part played in history by the human intellect ; but we may already say that it does not seem very logical to consider man's physical forces as productive forces and to exclude his mental powers. Neither Marx himself nor his followers seem ever to have made a thorough study of this question. Consciously or unconsciously, they shunned the inevitable logical conclusions. According to their theory, " the social, political and intellectual life of a society depends on the mode of production as necessitated by the wants of material life ". They seem to suppose that when the mode of production has reached a certain level, men's intelligence will be sufficiently advanced to understand the importance of certain discoveries, while the social system will be such as to make possible the general use of the newly discovered forces. The discoveries as well as their exploitation will therefore depend on the mode of production.

Though no proofs of the truth of this opinion have as yet been furnished, we shall for once assume that Marx is right and that his theory, as set forth in propositions 1-4, holds good. The result would be as follows : human knowledge and intelligence are determined by the conditions of production ; it is human intellect which, as we have seen, discovers new productive forces ; the development of these productive forces determines the conditions of production, which in turn determine the development of human intelligence . . . and so on. We are confronted by a circular course repeating itself to infinity, and no one can say which of these inter-dependent elements is the first or primary agency. Certainly not the productive forces, which in the whole process play a merely passive part.

Supposing the existence of such a circular course to be demonstrable, obviously none of the elements participating in the circular movement could be regarded as the one producing the movement, which could be produced only by a power outside the circle. To question which element of the circular movement is the first would be as intelligent as the question : Which was there first, the hen or the egg ?

Passages are to be found in Marx's works, which do not seem quite consistent with the theory developed in the fifteen propositions. Cunow, for instance, assures us that " according to Marx the mode of production is not determined solely by technique, but rather by three constituents, labour-power, nature and technique ". That does not seem to be exactly the same thing. Yet Marx never recanted or modified his theses, nor does Cunow contest their truth ; he calls them classical, quotes them *in extenso*, and constantly refers to them. The great majority of Marxists believe in the propositions, and even a few modern and slightly divergent opinions are nevertheless based on them.[1]

According to Marx's first proposition, the conditions of production, on which all other social phenomena

[1] There are, of course, slightly dissentient Socialists like Casimir von Kelles-Krauz, who, in an address at the fourth Sociological Congress at Brussels — published in the *Neue Zeit*, 1901, pp. 649, 684 — said : " Marx's definition is no longer up to date ; it does not correspond to the theory as it has since developed ". Yet his argument is less clear and less precise than Marx's own, and at bottom he only added new mistakes to those which are to be found in Marx's exposition. Kelles-Krauz based his opinions on an article by Karl Kautsky, " What is the Use and Purport of the Materialist Conception of History ? " — *Neue Zeit*, vol. xv. i, pp. 213, 228, 260 — an article that does not demonstrate anything except the author's deficiency in historical knowledge. Kautsky was carrying on a controversy against Belfort Bax, who rightly demanded that a theory of history ought to be large enough to explain human life.

depend, correspond to a certain stage of development of the productive forces. And when, as it is said in the fifth proposition, " arrived at a certain stage of their development, the material forces of production come into conflict with the existing conditions of production ", then the time has come for great historical changes to take place. If these two sentences have any meaning at all, they mean that the development of the productive forces is the true motive power, the basic fact in history. We certainly knew long ago that the discoveries of new productive forces, such as fire, steam-power, electricity, were most important events in human history and full of grave consequences. We did not need Marx and his theory to tell us that. What is new in his theory is the promotion of the productive forces to the rank of first cause.

Here again a Marxist might object : by development of the productive forces we do not only mean their discovery nor their being in general use ; the term is to be understood in a much larger sense. Expounding Marx's historical theory, Cunow says : " The constituents of the process of production, the co-operating productive forces are the first to change. . . ." And he hastens to explain that this not only means new technical methods, for " an increasing or decreasing application in the single branches of production of some well-known technical method, the replacement of one branch of production by another, or an increasing exploitation of the forces of nature or of labour, may essentially change the traditional mode of production. When the single constituents of the process of production change, the mode of production itself changes." [1] Of course ! For

[1] *Op. cit.* vol. ii. p. 309.

we are unable to see any difference between changes in the process of production and changes in the mode of production. It is quite clear and need not be affirmed that the mode — or the process, it is the same thing — of production changes through a change in its constituents, be it the workmen or the technique, that is, the methods. You may distinguish between productive forces on one hand — forces of nature, human force, machinery — and the mode of production, that is, their application, on the other. But if you say that a change in the application, the increasing or decreasing use of a productive force, the extension or limitation of a branch of production, is the same thing as the productive forces themselves, then we end in an inextricable confusion.[1]

[1] This self-deception by mere words is of perpetual occurrence in the works of this school. In another part of the same work Cunow says : " The productive forces do not determine the conditions of production, but they determine, according to the mode of their application, which is, in turn, determined by historical development, a particular method of production ".

We ask again, what is the difference between the mode of application and the method of production ? If I employ running water to make the wheels of a mill go round, this method of application is the mode of production ; and if I change my ways and first transform the water into electric power before applying it to the wheel, then this new mode of application is the new method of production. This self-deception by words makes the author overlook what is essential, namely, that it is not water-power or electricity that determine the method of production, but man who decides, according to his lights, which he is to employ, water or electricity. To be sure, Cunow adds that the application is determined by historical development. But to say this is to say nothing at all, for all events are determined by historical development.

A few lines further on Cunow says : " Only where men co-operate in the process of production in a certain fashion so that certain equal relations between their activities are produced, will equal conditions of production be the result ". Words, words, . . . the conditions of production are not a result of a certain co-operation of men in the processes of economic production, but this co-operation and the conditions of production are one and the same thing.

And to think that Cunow in the same passage reproaches Braunthal with overlooking the identity of two expressions !

If this were the case, all that Marx says about the productive forces would be meaningless. In a previous passage Cunow said : " According to Marx, the mode of production is the primary agency of all historical changes ". We thought it was the development of the productive forces. All this but serves to show how great is the confusion in terms as well as in the ideas of most Marxist philosophers.

The truth is that we have to see in history a tissue formed by innumerable and irregular reciprocal repercussions of different groups of phenomena upon each other.[1] Productive forces and conditions of production constantly influence and determine each other, just as the invention of new arms influences and determines warfare, and warfare continuously leads to the invention of new arms and new forms of military organisation. Yet only fools would pretend that the development of arms and of army organisation is the cause of war and the primary agency in military history.

The development of a productive force proceeds on the following lines : first, the new force is discovered by some person's mental activity ; after this, nothing happens, as a rule, for a long time ; then, sometimes, experts begin to study the new force and experiment with it ; until at last some bold and shrewd man gives it a trial and employs the force in economic production.[2] In early times, and in a primitive state of civilisation, the introduction of a new productive force is a great and

---

[1] As to the real nature of this reciprocity cf. pp. 104 *seq.*

[2] It was Matthew Boulton, the founder of wholesale industry in Birmingham, one of the greatest English merchants and capitalists, who first ventured to make use of Watt's invention in manufacture. Cf. Paul Mantoux, *La Révolution industrielle au 18ᵉ siècle* (Paris, 1906), p. 89, and J. L. and Barbara Hammond, *The Rise of Modern Industry* (London, 1925), ch. viii., " The Steam-Engine ", pp. 110-130.

bold step forward; in times when new devices and experiences are frequent, the introduction of a new force to industry may not require extraordinary courage; yet even then people will hesitate; and in many cases the step is never taken at all. For it means, in nearly all cases, the running of a certain risk, and the effects are sometimes incalculable. In some cases the development is a rapid one, in others it takes thousands of years. But be it rapid or slow, it is brought about by human insight and will-power. If the first experiment is successful, others will follow, and unless the existing conditions of production make it impossible, the use of the new force will become general.[1]

[1] There can be no doubt whatever that the procedure was exactly the same in primitive times. The first man who threw a bridle over a horse's neck, or who put a bull to the plough, was a very bold man who made an enormous step in advance; the man who used the first wooden tool to draw furrows across a field was an uncommonly intelligent fellow. It was probably done by several bold and intelligent men in different parts of the earth, and it may in certain cases have taken time before others followed their example, and still more time before the new practice became general. The imitative instinct of man played its part in assisting its coming into use; man's inertia and laziness set themselves against it.

All this happened in " the far abysm of time ", no record of which has come down to us; we cannot be sure that it was so, because we were not present when it happened; yet we may be logically certain of it. The primitive tribes, that are still to be found on this earth, have all long passed the first brute stage, and their civilisation seems static. We are unable to observe what would interest us more than anything else; the first beginnings of a new development are hidden from our eyes. The changes that occur in a primitive state of civilisation seem to be immeasurably slow and gradual; they are accomplished in a space of time of such length as to preclude observation.

Those changes and developments that we were able to observe, as, for instance, the North American hunting tribes turning to agriculture, occurred under exceptional conditions; they were due to the influence of the white race; there was neither discovery nor invention of a new force or method, but merely imitation. Research is confined to the static conditions of the existing primitives.

Theories on the transition from one state of civilisation to the other

The adherents of the Marxist theory, claiming to explain the course of history, say that it is the development of the productive forces which produces all other phenomena and developments. We have seen that this is by no means the case, but even if it were, how is the development of the productive forces to be accounted for ? Merely to use the words " development " or " evolution " is not explaining anything, it is only substituting one abstract term for another, and does not help us to see the concrete facts. As yet we have not been able to ascertain the exact way in which the great changes in men's political economy and civilisation are introduced ; still less could we discover the causes which called them forth.

All authors, Marxists as well as their opponents, agree that human economics comprise the activities by which men endeavour to satisfy their needs. We know that these activities have changed and developed since the first dawn of mankind, that different methods of production succeeded one another in the course of history. Here, three questions must necessarily arise. Why do men change their mode of production ; why do they not abide by one and the same mode of supplying their needs as the animals do ? The second question is : Why do they decide in favour of a particular method ? And the

and how they were brought about, are not wanting. Marxist authors devoted themselves to these studies with particular zeal, thinking to find ample proof of their theory in the history of primeval ages. All their conclusions, however, are hypothetical, resting upon analogies, probability and assumptions, and almost all are contested. One cannot be too much on guard against an argumentation which, from presumptive incidents and developments in unknown periods, draws conclusions for our own times. Moreover, the bulk of their theories on conditions and developments in prehistoric times are based on insufficient research, or on the assumption of facts which have since been proved to be unfounded.

third : How are the changes, the transitions from one mode of production to the other, to be accounted for ?

The answer to the first of these questions is obvious : because men are men, not foxes or bees, because even in the remotest past it has always been in their nature to look out for ever new ways of satisfying their needs. For this purpose they invented tools, constructed engines, and discovered and developed the forces of nature as well as their own forces, which after all are a part of nature. To keep this in mind will bring us somewhat nearer to understanding why and how those changes were brought about.

We have seen that all productive forces are discovered, developed and put to use by the human intellect. In like manner, the substitution in some branch of industry of machinery for manufacture by hand, the transition of a tribe from cattle-breeding to agriculture or the reverse, the expansion of industry and commerce in a country where the people hitherto lived chiefly on agriculture, are contrived by the human intellect. Intelligent and enterprising persons are the first to see which new methods promise better results than the old ones gave ; they will be the first to apply them, and other people will follow their lead. The more human intelligence develops, the more frequently some persons will be able to foresee that a certain branch or mode of production is going to become unprofitable and that it would be advisable to replace it in time by some better method or to proceed to the production of another kind of commodities. On the other hand, it is a fact of frequent occurrence to see the population of some town or village with a once flourishing industry suffer economic ruin because they cannot be induced to change their customary ways.

When mines become exhausted, when a branch of industry ceases to be profitable, when a group of producers are threatened with ruin by foreign competition, intelligent experts are needed to explore new ways. It is only a few years ago that the landowners in Germany were told by experts to give up producing rye, which they had mostly been growing and which had ceased to be profitable, and to grow wheat instead, or turn to horticulture and soil improvement.

Changes in the mode of production were generally brought about in this fashion in historic times, and there can be little doubt that it was the same in prehistoric ages.[1]

How dependent economic progress is upon intelligence, is shown by the fact that the innovation or the expedient may be mistaken, that the transition to a new branch of industry may be unsuccessful or, even if successful, may be accompanied by attendant phenomena injurious to society. All, in fact, depends on the insight and experience of the leading men.

Whenever the importance of human intellect in production and economics is pointed out to the adherents of the Materialist Conception of History, they invariably make answer that they know it well, that all their authors, from Marx and Engels to Franz Mehring and Heinrich Cunow, gave their attention to the fact, and that it has long been stated by them that intellectual phenomena are more or less important intermediate links in the different historical processes, but being of an ideological

[1] We have said " generally " because there are cases in which a change in the mode of production is enforced by a calamity, as, for instance, prolonged devastation of a country by war, enslavement of a nation by a foreign conqueror, or a change of trade routes. Such cases, however, may be considered as interruptions of the natural and regular development.

nature, they are rooted in the economic system and are ultimately created and determined by the conditions of production. In saying this, they have in view the so-called superstructure, political opinions, philosophy, science, etc. What they completely overlook is the fact that, as we have seen, the human mind plays the decisive part in the *basis*, in economics and production itself. As soon as we become aware of this, the whole theory crumbles, for the division into an economic basis and an intellectual superstructure becomes untenable.

This *proton pseudos* has been caused by Marx. By using the word " development " instead of " utilisation " or some similar term, Marx has, consciously or unconsciously, described the development of the productive forces as if it were more or less automatic ; and he certainly intended to say that all other phenomena of history, and particularly those which we call intellectual or psychic phenomena, are determined by this more or less automatic development.

Neither is it possible to interpret his doctrine in the sense that the growth of civilisation should be parallel to the development of the productive forces, or that their discovery and utilisation should be the most important fact in history. If that had been his meaning, his theory would have to be discussed from an altogether different point of view. It is no discovery that the differentiation of social life and culture proceeds simultaneously with the extension of man's power over the forces of nature ; we knew long ago that both developments are not only parallel, but intertwined and inter-dependent. History is the record of the continuous changes in men's relations to each other and to nature as well as of their moral and intellectual developments. The problem of which we are seeking the solution, is the causation of these changes. And with regard to this we can but repeat that, however important the part played by the productive forces may be, they are certainly not the primary agency by which these changes are brought about.

CHAPTER III

THE CONDITIONS OF PRODUCTION AND THE
IDEOLOGICAL SUPERSTRUCTURE

READING it carefully, Marx's theory, as expressed in the fifteen propositions, will be found to consist of four parts.

In the first part, proposition 1, it is said that the conditions of production correspond to a certain stage of the development of the productive forces.

The second part, propositions 2, 3 and 4, implies that the social, political and intellectual life of a society is based on the mode of production as necessitated by the needs of material life.

The third part, propositions 5-12, treats of the great historical revolutions.

The fourth part, propositions 13-15, gives the outlines of past history in accordance with the theory, and an outlook into the future of mankind.

We have seen that the first part does not hold good, especially if taken in a literal sense ; the productive forces being developed by man, the word " development " in Marx's sentence is to be understood in an active sense. Marx, moreover, neglected to investigate how this development, this increasing command of the productive forces, is brought about. Lastly, we have seen that the whole proposition is reversible, that we are quite as much entitled to say : the productive forces correspond to, and depend on, the development of the conditions of production.

The essential part is, however, the second ; and though the inadequate wording of the first part is not without importance for the second, yet the truth of the latter is not dependent on that of the first. It may be maintained as an independent theory and, if it could be proved, would be of decisive importance.

To the beginning, there can be no objection : " The conditions of production as a whole constitute the economic structure of society ". This is in fact only a paraphrase ; the same object is given another name. It is the second part of proposition 2 that contains the main issue of the matter : " The conditions of production are the material basis on which is raised a superstructure of laws and political institutions, and to which certain forms of political consciousness correspond ". Proposition 3, " The social, political and intellectual life of a given society depends on the mode of production as necessitated by the wants of material life ", is again only a paraphrase, an elucidation perhaps, of the preceding sentence ; and proposition 4, " It is not man's consciousness that determines the form of existence, but it is, on the contrary, the social forms of life which determine men's consciousness ", is in reality only another paraphrase of the same thought, couched in terms of the current philosophy of the time.[1]

In a limited sense, Marx's theory might be accepted. If we understand his words to imply that human society

---

[1] Proposition 4 might as well have been omitted. Marx, as Cunow has shown, put it there to assert his point of view — which may be traced back to the writings of L. A. Feuerbach — as against Hegel.

could not exist without economic production, or as he terms it, the " production of material life ", then it is perfectly true. There cannot be the slightest doubt that society depends upon production as its " real basis ".

But even though Marx says in another place,[1] " Men must be able to live in order to be able to make history. And to live one needs meat and drink, lodging, clothing and some other things ", his words are not so intended. He did not merely wish to imply that society depends on production for its existence. No one, in this case, would have contested his theory, but everyone would have replied : We knew this long ago ; man must live in order to be able to think and he must eat in order to be able to live. People who die of starvation are incapable of leading a political or intellectual life. What Marx wanted to say was not only that production is necessary, but that the mode of production is decisive ; that laws, constitutions, science, art and religion depend on the mode of production and are determined by it, and when the mode of production changes, everything else changes.

Air is also an essential condition of life ; we cannot make laws or write books if we are unable to breathe. If, however, some scientist should succeed in proving that the composition of the atmosphere has a decisive influence on our institutions and opinions, it would be a very important discovery. The problem we have to face is, therefore, whether the mode of economic production really has a definite and unmistakable influence on men's political and intellectual life, or not. That it has some influence cannot be denied, because everything

[1] *Deutsche Ideologie* (Historisch-Kritische Gesamtausgabe, Moskau und Leningrad, 1933), I. Abt. vol. v. p. 17.

that touches our life and existence in an important manner will, as a rule, have some effect on our opinions and actions ; but that is not the question. In the philosophical fourth proposition, Marx stated his meaning with perfect clarity ; translated into the language of our time, it would read as follows : economic activity and the social order do not result from man's intelligence, from their thoughts and feelings ; rather are their thoughts and feelings determined by their economic activity and the ensuing social order.

The proofs produced to substantiate this thesis were of two kinds. Either they were taken from prehistoric times, which is to say that one hypothesis was based on another hypothesis — the writers who did so assumed that people in prehistoric times lived in such and such a state, and then adduced their living in this state as a proof of the theory. Or, when taken from history, the proofs were furnished by sweeping statements conformable with the theory but not with reality, statements which had not been arrived at by inferences from the particular to the general, but the reverse.

Prehistory is a comparatively new science, and the theories and hypotheses on primitive civilisation are fluctuating and often contradictory. Marx and Engels based their ideas chiefly on Lewis Morgan's studies of the Iroquois and on Georg Ludwig von Maurer's work on the municipal and agrarian customs of the ancient Germans. Recent studies by explorers who have lived among the primitive tribes on the South Sea Islands, in Australia, in North and South America, have since led to views differing greatly from those held more than half a century ago. This is the regular and legitimate manner of scientific progress. But it is hardly admissible and certainly not conducive to knowledge, to adduce uncertain hypotheses based on incomplete research, as proofs of another hypothesis still more hazardous. We need only compare the very different views held on the totems and on matriarchy by Engels on one hand, and by Cunow on the other ; and when we confront both with the totally heterodox opinions of Professor Freud on the same subject, it is at once borne in upon us that science and research are moving here on precarious and uncertain ground. Moreover, authors habitually adduce only those facts which seem to tell in favour of their theory, setting aside or overlooking those which tell against it. Persons looking for proofs of a preconceived opinion are generally unable to see facts other than those which seem to support it.

It will seem advisable to confine our investigation to historical times, which is to say, to that part of human history which is tolerably well known to us. We shall admit that it is not always possible to draw a clear-cut line. There are nations and tribes in very different stages of civilisation living on this earth to-day, and we are probably justified in concluding that nations which have now attained a high level of culture once lived under conditions similar to those which we find among the primitive races of our day. In some cases we are even able to prove this, as records are not wanting in which the habits and customs of these nations in bygone times are depicted. Our essential point being, however, to find out the true causes of the changes which took place in the course of their history, it is clearly our first task to state the facts, the exact course taken by events. We certainly must first know how all this came about before we can tell why it happened. And the difficulty of acquiring this knowledge is generally in proportion to the length of time that has passed since the event.

The authors who tried to furnish proofs for the Marxist theory, generally chose a less laborious method. They contented themselves with stating that an economic change of some kind or other took place at a certain time, and that, several years or decades or centuries later, a change took place in the institutions or in the ideas of the same people, whereupon they unhesitatingly declared that the second change was caused by the first. Their conclusion was invariably : *post hoc ergo propter hoc.* They utterly neglected to examine the many intermediate links necessary to build up the chain of causation. They were perfectly satisfied to assume a possible connection, provided that it suited their theory. Like all persons who reason at haphazard, they were sometimes right in their assumptions, because economic changes generally have important consequences, though they were more often wrong. There is nothing easier than to draw general conclusions from the superficial knowledge of a few facts, whereas it takes an enormous amount of time and work thoroughly to study even a relatively short period and really to trace the causation of even a few important events.

One may call the former method that of the elimination — based on ignorance — of the intermediate links. It is employed in daily life, in politics as well as in history. Authors like Gobineau, Houston Stewart Chamberlain, Oswald Spengler and many others make constant use of it. It is regularly employed by lawyers endeavouring to deflect the course of justice.

Historic science requires the same conscientious

34

examination of all available facts as penal justice. It is, of course, inevitable in this science as in any other to make use of generalisations, to survey and compress whole periods or movements into a few abstract sentences, but, as in every other science, such summaries must be based on an exact knowledge and verification of the single facts and events. That is to say, they must be arrived at by the inductive method, whereas in the cases mentioned above, some sudden flash of thought, some ready-made theory is proclaimed as a new truth, whereupon the author looks out for facts to substantiate it, accepts them untested and arranges them so as to suit his idea. A man is enabled, by this means, to say brilliant and sensational things and sometimes he may even intuitively strike on a truth. As a rule, however, his deductions will be erroneous and misleading. And, above all, it is impossible to prove anything in this way.

To give a few instances : in Karl Kautsky's article " What is the Use and Purport of the Materialist Conception of History ? "[1] Puritanism in England is explained as follows : " The transition from a natural to a monetary system of economy ", says the author, " causes the lower classes to fall a prey to a sombre puritanism." Why it should be so is not explained. The mere fact that the same transition in other countries did not conduce to Puritanism, should have sufficed to make it clear to Kautsky and others that Puritanism has nothing to do with this economic change, but has to be traced back to some other origin. In France it was chiefly the nobility that became Protestant and took to a sombre view of human life. Moreover, as Belfort Bax alleged against Kautsky, the two phenomena are

[1] Cf. p. 19.

separated by an interval of several centuries. The transition to a monetary system of economy began in England in the eleventh and was completed in the fourteenth century, whereas Puritanism appeared towards the end of the sixteenth century and, as in France, could be traced back to the spiritual influence of John Calvin.

In another passage of the same article we find the following statement: " The Romans developed no civilisation of their own, because when they made their conquests they were barbarians. Moreover, the economic development of Rome was already on the decline." Let us consider the second sentence first. If the accumulation of immense riches, the transition to ever more complex economic institutions, are to be regarded as symptoms of decline, then the economic system of Great Britain was in constant decline during the whole of the nineteenth century. If they are not to be considered as such, then the political economy of the ancient Romans was in constant progress until the second century after Christ. We may look upon it as a decline from a moral point of view, if we choose to consider the economic system supported by vigorous peasants in the early days of the republic as the climax. Anybody is free, of course, to decide which system he prefers ; but peasant political economy is not usually attended by a high culture. Nothing, moreover, could be more preposterous than to declare that the Romans were barbarians in the second century B.C., which was the period in which they conquered Greece and the countries tinged by Greek culture. The Romans have sometimes been called barbarians in comparison with the Greeks because they did not produce an art and a philosophy properly their own. The word was meant in a relative sense. When we call a person of our own time a barbarian because he is not interested in poetry and art, we do not mean to say that he is a savage. A nation which produced institutions and laws that have become a model to posterity, which developed the highest military art and a refined luxury of life, cannot be called " barbaric " in an ethnological or historical sense, but rather a nation which has reached one of the highest states of civilisation known to history.

We might take no account of an author like Kautsky, whose conclusions are generally ill-considered and whose historical knowledge is extremely superficial, if it were not for the conspicuous part he plays among the followers of the theory. But even authors of real merit are apt to declare two phenomena as standing in the relation of cause and effect solely because one was posterior to the other. Professor Franz Oppenheimer, for instance, writes in his *Skizze der sozialökonomischen Geschichtsauffassung* [1] that the transformation of the warlike and insubordinate French nobles into the cringing courtiers of Louis XIV was due to the introduction of the monetary system into France. For, says Oppenheimer, they now no longer had need of an armed retinue to extort as much as possible from their tenants ; what they now needed was the assistance and favour of the court. The real course of events, however, was quite different. To begin with, we must again state that the transition to the monetary system had taken place at a much earlier period. Moreover, the dues which the tenants once paid to their lords in kind, never had pressed heavily upon them ; the dues in money which had since replaced them had, owing to the depreciation of money

[1] *Vierteljahrsschrift für wissenschaftliche Philosophie und Soziologie,* Jgg. 27, 1903.

after the discovery of the New World, become ridiculously small; they frequently amounted to no more than a few centimes. The landlords certainly needed no armed men to collect taxes that were purely nominal.[1] Abuses and extortions were no doubt more or less frequent, but on the whole, the peasants were the gainers and the landlords the losers. During the religious wars of the sixteenth century, the nobles loaded themselves with heavy debts and were utterly ruined. Though peasants and townsmen suffered the same fate, they were in a position to work their way up, whereas special laws forbade the nobles to do this. No nobleman was allowed to cultivate more than four yoke of land himself. He was a warrior and had to remain one; his only way out was to enlist and hope for preferment.

Moreover, the revolution which Professor Oppenheimer has in view, affected only the grandees, who formed a very small part, not even *one* per cent, of the French nobility. Whereas the mass of the French nobles had been ruined by the religious wars, the grandees had profited by them; they had acquired great riches and become more powerful than before. They still kept strong armed suites in the first decades of the seventeenth century, and I do not suppose that Oppenheimer thinks monetary economy was introduced

[1] To give an instance : Philippe Messeau, who, as a vassal of the barons of Richelieu, worked the domain of Richelieu, in a document still existing, acknowledges " with due reverence to owe to the Lady of Richelieu " — mother of the great Cardinal — " from this domain the sum of fifteen sous per annum ". Cf. Gabriel Hanotaux, *Histoire du Cardinal de Richelieu*, vol. i. p. 47. Hundreds of similar cases might be cited, and it would be wrong to assume that all the lords of the manor were oppressors. The current notions of conditions in France during the Middle Ages are to a large extent erroneous. It was d'Avenel's masterly work, *Histoire économique de la propriété, des salaires, etc. en France* (Paris, 1893 *sqq.*), that first shed light on this subject.

into France as late as that. The grandees were, and always had been, obnoxious and dangerous to Royalty, and Richelieu therefore determined to destroy their power. He carried out his design with iron will and ruthless energy; he deprived them of their privileges, forced them to dismiss their suites and broke their spirit. They made a feeble attempt to regain their power in the rebellion called the Fronde; but it was an absurd rebellion, easily quashed by Mazarin and the royal army. Being, however, in possession of enormous estates and numerous strongholds, they might again have become dangerous under a weak monarch, and it was for this reason that Louis XIV, steadily pursuing the same policy, constrained the members of the highest aristocracy — but only these — to live at his court. When one of them was appointed governor of a province, he was nevertheless not allowed to leave the neighbourhood of Versailles; he had to send some lesser nobleman as his deputy, his *lieutenant-général*, into the capital of the province.

Political, economic and purely personal causes cooperated to bring about this result, as is always the case in history. It is noteworthy, however, that the political and economic developments were in striking contrast, for the great aristocracy had become particularly rich and powerful, and for this reason was ruined politically. The smaller nobility, to the number of eighty or a hundred thousand — whereas the court noblesse was made up of a few hundred families — had not the means to go to court; they remained in the provinces, and many of them were abjectly poor. The court did not grant them any assistance in exacting money from their tenants; on the contrary, the civil officers of the royal government did their utmost to curtail the feudal rights of the nobility.

The great nobles who lived on the bounties of the court and depended on the King's good graces, attached little value to these rights ; it was the deputies of the highest nobility who, in 1789, moved the abolition of all feudal privileges. The fact that in other countries the transition to monetary economy had no such consequences, should have made Oppenheimer, as well as Kautsky, think twice before ascribing the decay of the French aristocracy to this change. All that he writes on the subject is pure imagination ; it proves that even prominent authors fall into error by making sweeping statements on historical events without sufficient knowledge of the details. We might cite several similar mistakes from his article.

To quote another instance : Professor Antonio Labriola, in his treatise, *La Conception matérialiste de l'histoire* (2nd ed., Paris, 1928), tries to explain why the aborigines in America did not attain a high state of civilisation. He finds the reason very simple ; there were in America, before its discovery by Europeans, no cereals except maize and no animal which could be tamed except the llama. It was Europeans who introduced horned cattle, horses, donkeys, wheat, sugar-cane, oranges, etc. Now, though wheat was lacking, there was not only maize in America, but potatoes, peanuts and other fruits, and though it is perfectly true that Europeans introduced several kinds of domestic animals, as well as cereals and other useful plants, they did not introduce the bovine race. Vast herds of bison filled the North American plains, which the Red Indians might have tamed just as the Europeans tamed the European bison, the negroes the buffalo, the Mongols the yak. Those who lived in the Arctic regions might have domesticated the reindeer as did the Laplanders and many Asiatic tribes. However, they were not capable of this ; it was not among their gifts. Besides this curious oversight, Labriola seems entirely to forget that, in spite of these deficiencies, the Mayas, the Aztecs, the Incas and other peoples developed what cannot be termed otherwise than a comparatively high state of civilisation ; and nobody can tell what level they might have reached, had not the development been cut short. In the two last-named cases it was cut off by the Europeans, who destroyed it.

Thus we find the same faulty reasoning occurring again and again. A conclusion that agrees with the theory is prematurely drawn without making any thorough and extensive study of the problem in hand ; [1] some sweeping statement is made which is neither subjected to any close examination, nor is any attempt made to obtain confirmatory proof. No reasonable scientist, perceiving that upon mixing certain substances with nitre there follows an explosion, will forthwith conclude that nitre invariably causes explosions. He will first examine whether mixing nitre with other substances has the same effect, and even if this should be the case, he will still be far from certain that nitre is the sole cause ; he may find that a higher temperature than usual, or an exposure of the mixture to the sun was the real cause ;

[1] The assurance with which these conclusions are drawn, borders sometimes on the ludicrous. Franz Mehring, for instance, in his essay on "Historical Materialism" (printed as an appendix to the same author's *Lessing-Legende*, Stuttgart, 1893) on p. 347 says that "the fountains of Versailles reappear in the dramatic pieces of Corneille". Now, the famous tragedies of Corneille were all written and performed in the first half of the seventeenth century, whereas the basins and fountains of Versailles were only completed between 1672 and 1682. Corneille died at this time, a man half-forgotten by the court and the French public. His tragedies reflect the period of Richelieu and Louis XIII, who held court at the Louvre, not that of Louis XIV at Versailles—a totally different period.

and even if he should find that nitre was indeed the substance that started the explosion, he will try to penetrate the problem and investigate whether nitre alone was sufficient to start it, or whether other conditions were required, and other factors must co-operate in order to produce this result. A conscientious physician, desirous to know the effect of some medical remedy, will follow exactly the same method ; and so will a cultivator who wants to find out the true cause of a good or bad harvest. Clearly these problems are very simple compared to those set by history, wherein all phenomena are infinitely complex, because millions of persons and events co-operate to produce new events or to create a certain state of things. Only the closest investigation of the facts and their causal concatenation, the study of countless details and the comparison of events and situations with numerous similar events and situations equally well known, may possibly enable us to understand events or a period of the past. Yet, confronted by this intricate and complex matter, where all is uncertain and exact knowledge most difficult, men are ready, whenever one of two events is posterior to the other, to declare without further ado that the second was caused by the first.

Reading the essays in which Marxist authors tried to support their theory, one is nearly always confronted by this superficial and irresponsible method of procedure. The most hazardous and the most erroneous conclusions are drawn from the fact that two events were approximately simultaneous or succeeded one another. In this fashion, and by summing up in a few vague sentences, without giving even a faint notion of the world of events which such a space of time really represents, one may advance almost any opinion, nearly any statement. One generalisation is adduced to support the other, and both have no foundation in fact. Nearly a hundred years ago, Cournot warned students to employ this method with caution, when he wrote, "Analysis leads to the elimination of errors, synthesis — meaning generalisation — accumulates them ".[1]

There can be no doubt whatever that political economy and the forms of production have far-reaching consequences and are of the greatest importance in history. The life and existence of the individual and of society depend upon them. The opinions as well as the moral, and still more the political, attitude of single individuals and of society as a whole are largely influenced by their economic interests. The question with which we are confronted, however, is whether it is true that the sum-total of intellectual, cultural and political phenomena in any community not only depends for its existence upon economic production, but is, in all its modifications, determined by it. Are all such phenomena indeed but a superstructure? Not in the sense that there must first be economic production before other developments are possible — nobody will deny this — but in the larger sense according to which the mode of production determines all other manifestations of the community? [2]

[1] A. A. Cournot, *Essai sur le fondement de nos connaissances* (Paris, 1851), ch. xvii., " De l'Analyse et de la Synthèse ", vol. ii. p. 95.

[2] There are passages in Marx's works which seem to suggest that he thought other influences possible. In the draft mentioned on p. 15 we find the following note : " One must begin with the determination — in a subjective as well as in an objective sense — tribes, races ". It is to be regretted that we do not know what exactly Marx may have meant by these words ; they seem almost to suggest a broader interpretation of the theory. We cannot, however, be in any way certain of this ; whereas it is quite certain that in the accepted doctrine there is small question of race and tribes, but only of the forces and conditions of production.

43

Marxist authors do not always clearly see this difference. They go on repeating that men must first eat, drink, find lodging and clothes, before they are able to think, to write poetry, to display political activities, etc.[1] These are truisms. It is, as we saw before, an incontestable truth that economic production is the condition of all other activities. These authors mistake the condition for the cause.

" Every activity of man ", says Marx, " every quality, every impulse of his develops into a need." [2] All the activities of the individuals as well as of organised communities are devoted to the satisfaction of such needs. Every such need impels men to actions by which he hopes to satisfy it. Frequently, however, these actions have unexpected consequences, very different from what was anticipated. It also happens that the true source of these actions and of their consequences is either forgotten, or even in some cases never was consciously appreciated at all.

The instinct of self-preservation is at the root of life ; the need of food or hunger is the form in which it most frequently makes itself felt, impelling men to countless activities, some of which are quite simple, whereas others are of a very complex kind. The need to guard oneself against the inclemencies of weather and climate, against illness and dangers of any kind, are manifestations of the same instinct. The manifold activities to which men are driven by these needs have developed into what we call men's economics and much else besides.

The sexual instinct, no less important, serving to

---

[1] Franz Mehring, for instance, makes exactly the same mistake on p. 446 of the essay quoted on p. 42.

[2] *Die heilige Familie*, Litt. Nachlass, vol. ii. p. 227.

maintain the race, exercises a powerful influence on individuals through the greater part of their lives ; an influence which often tends to increase their economic activity, but in countless other cases impels them to actions that have nothing whatever to do with it or even run counter to it.

The same thing may be said of the desire for power and of vanity, both of which play an important part in social life and history. Maybe, they are at bottom mere modifications of the instinct of self-preservation ; there can, however, be no doubt that, in private as well as in social and political life, they play a specific and very conspicuous part.

The more simple and primitive the state of a society, the more openly these instincts will dominate its social and economic life. With the differentiation implied by growing civilisation, various new impulses will develop, while those primary instincts often undergo strange modifications.

This is one of the reasons why the followers of the Materialist Theory of History prefer to evidence it by describing the institutions and habits of primitive nations and times : primitive states of civilisation admit of a limited application of the theory.

The more primitive an individual or a community, the greater obviously will be the part which mere physical necessity plays in their lives. The more society develops, the more differentiated the institutions and habits of men become, the more desires and needs spring up, which have nothing in common with those simple primitive needs and with the activities destined to supply them. Hence, a theory based on the study of primitive tribes would, even if true of them, not therefore necessarily be applicable to our own times. It must, however, be borne in mind that even when applied to a primitive society, the theory contains only a partial truth.

Let us, for instance, take a hunting tribe which explorers have had opportunity to observe, and study its habits and its mental attitude. The intellectual life of the tribe consists, in the first place, of experiences in hunting, cooking, feeding, building canoes and primitive houses. The elder persons give instructions to the young concerning hunting and warfare ; reports, perhaps songs, of adventures in hunting and war, are made and repeated. There is, moreover, the knowledge of certain traditions, opinions and customs, having their origin partly in the tribal mode of life as hunters, partly in sex, and to a large extent in special experiences of the tribe or of single individuals belonging to it. All these traditions, customs and experiences are a compound result of the way of living and the character of the race ; and we may note at once that in order to explain the character of the race, we should have to trace it back to remote and unknown times and to causes hidden from our knowledge. A fourth, and very essential part of the intellectual life of the tribe, consists in religious views, belief in spirits and magic, rites and customs of many kinds.

Marxist authors have made the most desperate attempts to explain religion and religious life. Cunow has written a book to prove the economic origin of all religion ; yet he succeeded only in proving that the economic life of primitive races is, to a certain extent, reflected in their religious ideas and imagination, which is perfectly natural. Hunting will always be present in the thoughts of members of a hunting tribe, cattle in those of a people of cattle-breeders and warfare in those

46

of a warrior nation. But this does not explain anything.

The theories of primitive religions are extremely divergent ; [1] yet all will probably agree in saying that when men begin to believe in spirits and in gods they are seeking for the causes of unexplained events and occurrences. It is their need of causality, of knowing the why and wherefore of things, combined with their scant experience of causation, that leads to these assumptions. Man cannot help discovering that he is not all-powerful ; on the contrary, he is constantly made to feel that he is weak and powerless ; countless events are taking place without or even against his will ; he is threatened and often destroyed by dangers, and good comes to him which is not of his own doing. The world in which he lives is not made by him ; sun and stars rise and set, the seasons pass without his being able to interfere ; a storm destroys his village, a stroke of lightning sets it ablaze ; he falls suddenly ill ; he passes his nights in terror, he hears the roar of wild animals

---

[1] Of all these theories the most plausible seems to be the one set forth by Gabriel Tarde in his *Lois des imitations* (Paris, 1890), vol. i. p. 292. He is of opinion that the exalted respect paid to the father and progenitor led to the worship of the dead, that the terrific beasts of prey of those times were regarded as demons, which again later on led to the deification of domestic animals, lastly that imposing strangers were deified. Tarde believes that it was the powers of destruction which first struck the imagination of primitive man and were magnified by it, whereas the belief in kind and creative spirits was of later origin. Tarde seems, however, to overlook the important part which the stars and sex must have played in primitive religious thought. It is unthinkable that the aspect of the rising sun, which, moreover, delivered the savage from the dangers and terrors of night and darkness, should not have impressed him with the feeling of a supernatural presence.

It is also necessary to bear in mind that all theories as to the origin of primitive religions are but hypotheses, which may be more or less plausible but are not demonstrable. It is impossible for us to know anything about it with certainty.

prowling around his hut ; the morning sun delivers him from his fear ; he sees the wonders of procreation, of the ripening fruits, the whole spectacle of life and death . . . the wish to explain all this, increased by hope and fear, created primitive religions.[1]   In the image of the soul which he felt or believed to exist within his own body, he ascribed a soul to all possible objects, living and inanimate.   He had, of course, but a dim idea of this " soul " ; the main point is, that he supposed a will active behind appearances, a will that might be kindly disposed or ill-intentioned.[2]   The fact that, beside the deified dead and the animals, early divinities were invariably either celestial bodies or beings impersonating sex and procreation, is ample proof that religious ideas are mainly due to the overwhelming impression which the phenomena of nature made on the primitive mind, whereas their connection with the

[1]   " Religion ", said Friedrich Engels, " is nothing but the fantastic reflection in men's minds of those external forces which control their daily life, a reflection in which terrestrial forces assume the form of supernatural forces.   In the beginning of history, it was the forces of nature that were at first so reflected and, in the course of further evolution, they underwent the most manifold and varied personifications amongst the various peoples " (Engels, *Anti-Dühring*, pp. 353-4).

This is more or less the same thing.   Only Engels, who was no penetrating thinker, did not see that his explanation is flatly contradictory to his theory, according to which religion, as part of the ideological superstructure, is determined by the mode of production.

[2]   " There is no ' chance ' for primitive man, no calamity can be casual ; his urge to find a cause for every occurrence is so strong that he invariably looks for a reason which, in his eyes, is perfectly rational ", Lucien Lévy-Bruhl, *La Mentalité primitive* (Paris, 1912), p. 27.   As for the intellectual life of the primitives, cf. the same author's *L'Âme primitive* (Paris, 1927), and Herbert Spencer, *Principles of Sociology* (London, 1876–96), vol. i. In all these works, however, it is more the way of thinking of the Primitives that is analysed, whereas we are chiefly interested in examining the contents of their thoughts and imagination ; we want to know to which subjects their attention is given.   Yet even their way of thinking is rooted in their nearness to nature, the undeveloped state of their minds, not in their mode of production.

mode of production is quite subordinate. Man, of course, turns to these Powers, imploring their protection, their assistance in war, invoking their blessings on the harvest and on his herds. Yet the star and sex-worships which were predominant through an immeasurable flux of time, are in no way connected with, or dependent on, the mode of production. The Sun and the Moon are the gods of the primitive savages as well as of civilised merchants and tillers of the soil. Whatever strikes man's imagination, or appeals to his emotions, appears in his religious ideas and imagery. All the evidence we have of primitive nations shows that, though food and the necessities of life play a much larger part in their lives than they do in ours, they do not play any exclusive part in their religious ideas. Life after death they imagined to be an improved and embellished continuance of their present life. What else was to be expected? Surely this belief does not prove anything in favour of Marx's theory.[1] The belief in a life after death which plays so important a part in the religious ideas of primitive as well as civilised nations, has nothing to do with economics or with the mode of production. It is a result of man's intense desire to live, which is more or less the same under any conditions and whatever the mode of production may be. The animals, though possessed of the same desire, lack the necessary imagination and are therefore unable to conceive a life after death. With men it is different, and as soon as this idea has once taken root, it becomes an important factor, invading all provinces of life and influencing economics to no small extent.

[1] At other times, for instance in the Christian era, the conception and the images of a future life are quite different, certainly stand in no relation to the mode of production and may, perhaps, be regarded as a perpetuation of an idealised monastic life.

We can but repeat that our knowledge of the people who lived in those remote times is very limited, yet the most hazardous assertions have been made as to their habits and institutions.

A great deal has been said and written by Marxist sociologists on the position of woman among the primitive races, and in accordance with their theory this had to be explained by economic reasons. They were ready to admit that Engels was mistaken in affirming that woman always held an honoured position in prehistoric times, because facts too manifestly proved the contrary, but the exceptions were easily accounted for.

" Nomadic and hunting tribes look down on woman ", says Cunow, " because women are of no use in hunting and cattle-breeding and unfit for the fighting in which these warlike peoples are constantly involved." In the ages of matriarchy, however, which coincided with those of early agriculture, it was woman who wielded the authority ; her services, being indispensable in agriculture, enabled her to gain a preponderant position in the economic system. Thus Edward Carpenter and many others. Cunow, expressing the same opinion, refers to a work by Professor Grosse on the relations between economics and the constitution of the family.[1] Grosse's conclusions, however, are very different. He says that, in primitive races, family ties and kinship are frequently based on descent from the mother's side ; and so are the rights of inheritance. But this does not constitute matriarchy. Matriarchy, which means the supremacy of the mother and woman's rule, is a rare exception even in agricultural tribes and nations. It is

[1] Ernst Grosse, *Die Formen der Familie und die Formen der Wirtschaft*, Freiburg und Leipzig, 1896.

to be found among the Hurons and the Iroquois in North America, the Garos in India and a few Malay tribes,[1] and there is nothing, says Grosse, to justify the opinion that it can ever have been general. Yet, even if this should have been the case, it was, in spite of " woman's economic superiority ", very soon superseded by the patriarchate, the supremacy of man. Succession and kinship may be based on descent from the mother's side, for the natural reason that only this descent is visibly evident and unquestionable, yet this institution or custom is independent of position and power ; the mother derives no rights from it ; as Grosse says, " the inheritance reverts to the mother's side, but the mother herself is only a part of the inheritance ". [2]

Agriculture seems to have come into existence in some such manner as the following. The women of hunting and cattle-breeding tribes naturally collected wild fruits wherever they were available ; in fertile regions they probably did so regularly, thus acquiring notions of seed and harvest. In course of time they began to assist nature in her work, planting fruit trees

[1] Spencer makes mention of matriarchy among the Kokks in the Himalayas, of the better social position of women on the Tonga Islands, and a few other cases. Cf. H. Spencer, *Principles of Sociology*, vol. iii. p. 414. These isolated cases serve only to prove that, notwithstanding identical conditions of production, we may find the most widely varying ideas and institutions.

[2] Exaggerated opinions as to the expansion and importance of the matriarchal state are due to J. J. Bachofen's work, *Das Mutterrecht, eine Untersuchung über die Gynaekokratie der alten Welt nach ihrer religiösen und rechtlichen Bedeutung* (Stuttgart, 1861). Bachofen's conclusions are, almost without exception, based on passages from Greek and Roman authors who habitually resorted to rumours and hearsay, had no idea of critical investigation, and whose reports cannot be verified. Bachofen's theory is not confirmed by scientific research.

His work is important, because he opened out new paths and was the pioneer of comparative jurisprudence.

and nutritive grains. It was obvious that when a tribe lost their cattle through an epidemic or because a stronger tribe took their herds, they would fall back on this incipient agriculture ; or perhaps some region of exuberant fertility invited them to profit by it. If such a change gave the women a temporary importance and perhaps even a show of superiority, this did not and could not last. Men were stronger and quite naturally appropriated the fruits as well as the rights. For it was not economics or the mode of production, but bodily strength and physical superiority that enforced the law.

It is a fact that the great majority of agricultural tribes and nations do not treat their women any better than the nomadic tribes do. With most African tribes, woman was and is no better than a slave. Among the Romans as well as among the ancient Germans her legal position, at least, was that of a slave. In all eastern countries, woman tills and cultivates the land to this day, yet we do not find that her work has conferred upon her any rights or honours. In some parts of the Balkans, woman is to this day bound to kiss her husband's hand.

A further objection to Cunow is that the regular occupation of women in the Alpine countries, in Norway and in many other regions, proves that woman is very capable of assisting in cattle-breeding and even of taking a leading position in this branch of economics. If, therefore, a great many nomad tribes excluded her from taking any part in it, there must have been other reasons for such treatment. The main fact, however, is that in agricultural nations woman does the principal work and is despised ; in nomad tribes she is strictly forbidden to join in the work and is also despised. The conclusion to be drawn from this fact is obvious.[1]

Even apart from all these historical facts that prove the contrary, the very idea that, because women worked in the fields, they should have been honoured and given a ruling position in the community, is preposterous. When and where in history has work as such been conducive to an honourable position and to power ? Even in our time, the honour that is paid to it is very limited ; it exists, generally speaking, rather in words than in reality. At all times, work was imposed on women and slaves and on feeble and insignificant people ; it was extremely useful, but it was not honoured. Honoured were the strong who appropriated the goods which the working people produced. The Marxists, of course, know this well enough ; they even lay great stress upon

[1] This state of things is, however, not without exceptions. Some warlike nomads, as, for instance, Arab tribes, respect their women and grant them civil rights. Cf. Richard Burton, *A Pilgrimage to Mekkah and Medinah* (London, 1893–4), vol. i.

Even among closely related tribes, living under exactly similar conditions of production, women are treated in the most varying fashion. Of the Indians on the western coast of North America, the Kootchin, the Californian tribes and the Hidas despise their womenfolk and ill-treat them ; the Hootka treat them fairly well but consider them as drudges, whereas the women of the Tlinkit are honoured by the men and exert great influence upon them. Cf. Grosse, *op. cit.* Only by close investigation — if this should be possible — could we perhaps learn what economic, sexual, religious or purely personal causes, such as, possibly, the appearance among the Tlinkit of a woman of superior gifts, may have produced these diversities of custom. We are by no means attempting to deny that economic causes may have such consequences. We only want to state the truth that there are many other motives and causes besides those of an economic nature, and that only after a close inquiry into the nature of every single case can we be in a position to say which motive or cause has, in this particular case, been decisive. In most cases we shall probably find that several varying motives combined and co-operated to bring about the result.

Kinship, clans and the status of the family as a whole which has played and still plays such an important part in the life of primitive tribes, has, as Grosse says, always been supported by economic facts, but not created by economic causes. For it originates in sex.

it. How, then, can they pretend that the agricultural work which was done by women gave them authority and power ? They cannot have it both ways. Those who set forth this opinion, neither examined the facts nor bestowed any serious thought on the problem, being ready to accept any solution, provided that an economic reason was given.

Anybody who is able to see things as they are, unhampered by the blinkers of a preconceived opinion, will arrive at the natural conclusion that man, being physically stronger than woman and in many cases, though certainly not always, mentally her superior, dominated and exploited her, and put her in a subordinate position, as the stronger have done with the weaker since time immemorial. They certainly did so in the savage state and they often do so still. Economic abilities were not of the least avail against this. On the contrary, those who possessed economic abilities, soon became a chosen object of domination and exploitation. There is only one exception to this rule. When those who were economically proficient, succeeded in making themselves strong by efficient organisation — which was possible only in comparatively advanced times — then only could they hope to enjoy the produce of their work. In all other cases they invariably sooner or later succumbed to invasion and spoliation by warlike barbarians whose economic abilities were far below theirs. Ancient and mediaeval history is a continuous example of this. If woman proved her economic value by tilling the fields, sowing and reaping, she was the more certain to be exploited and degraded to the position of a slave ; and if, in the rare cases of matriarchy, warriors who might easily have done so, refrained from exploiting women

54

and even submitted to gynaecocracy, there must have been reasons for this unknown to us, which certainly were not of an economic, but rather of a sexual or religious nature.

There is nothing more absurd and illogical than to accept far-fetched explanations of the subjection of women, since the reasons are palpable and obvious. The Marxist explanation is particularly inapplicable to the period in question. In an advanced state of civilisation, under the strict rule of equitable laws, when the use of force and physical power is an exception and no longer the rule, it is possible for women to dominate over men by economic superiority or even by personal ability. Even then it is by no means the rule, since the natural physical and sexual superiority of man takes effect in spite of all laws and all economics. In primitive times the domination of women owing to economic superiority, was simply impossible.

Physical achievements and warlike qualities stand in high esteem even in our time ; it is by no means uncommon to see them gaining more applause and having more success than intellectual or economic abilities. How much more must this have been the case in times when physical superiority meant everything.

Women owe the equal rights or at least the more honourable position which they have gradually obtained, not to any economic cause but, as Grosse rightly says, to a purely spiritual movement, namely, to the Christian religion. The Christian doctrine that the immortal soul living within him, was man's true and lasting self, destined to eternal life, changed the valuation of the individual. Woman's real self, her soul, was as priceless as man's ; the Son of God had died on the Cross to redeem it.

Owing to this creed, woman became, as far as religion was concerned, the equal of man, just as the slave for the same reason became the equal of his master whom Antiquity had considered to be so immeasurably superior to him. Moreover, the worship of the Virgin, by exalting one woman, conferred a new dignity on the whole sex. The adoration of the Virgin, combined with the new idea of Caritas or Divine Love, led to an estimation and even over-estimation of woman which, based as it was on sexual and religious feelings, had lasting effects on our civilisation. It became a dominating power in men's nerve-centres and was sublimated into an idea.[1] " Chivalrous " is to this day the word for what is considered the becoming attitude towards women, in remembrance of the period in which this new custom was introduced.

In this place, any Marxist would object that the spiritual movement of Christendom was itself due to economic causes. According to the Marxist theory, the rise of Christendom can be rationally explained by the economic misery in the Roman Empire, which made mankind look forward to a blissful state in a future life as a redeeming hope, while the union of so many nationalities in one and the same Empire and the free accordance and subsequent extension of Roman Citizenship had made an international ideal acceptable to the inhabitants of the antique world.

The propagation and diffusion of the Christian religion offers an excellent opportunity to apply, so to speak, a crucial test to the truth of the Marxist theory of history.

The diffusion of Christianity in the Old World was

[1] Cf. Eduard Wechssler, *Das Kulturproblem des Mittelalters. I.: Minnesang und Christentum*, Halle, 1909.

accomplished, approximately, in the time from the middle of the first century to the twelfth century, that is, more than a thousand years.

It must be said, in the first place, that the economic misery which, it is asserted, was one of the sources from which the Christian religion derived its origin, did not exist. The larger part of the population of the Roman Empire were at no time so well off and happy as during the first two centuries after the fall of the Republic. Never before had the ancient world enjoyed such a long and unbroken period of peace ; the imperial governors were not allowed by the emperors to exploit and oppress the provinces, as the Roman aristocracy had done under the republican regimen, and riches and general well-being increased accordingly. During this time, the Christian religion expanded slowly and gradually over the Empire.[1]

About the end of the second century after Christ, this general prosperity began to decline. Continuous civil wars brought about increasing misery, made worse by invasions of barbaric tribes. The military organisation of the Empire decayed and crumbled. The so-called migration of peoples, which at bottom was but an accelerated influx of the barbarians who until now had

[1] This fact will be better understood by bearing in mind that the first centuries of our era were a time of religious reaction against the unbelief and scepticism which were in vogue in the higher strata of antique society. New kinds of worship chiefly of Oriental origin, with strange mysteries and new doctrines of salvation, spread over the Empire. The Christian doctrine benefited by this general tendency.

This, of course, is no explanation. We may state a number of similar alternating waves of belief and unbelief in Antiquity, in the Middle Ages, and in modern times. The same fluctuations are to be found in the Islamic world. It would be extremely difficult — unless one is easily contented with the first superficial explanation at hand — to find out the real causes of these movements.

been repelled by Roman legions, completed the general ruin. The civil population of the Empire was, at this period, perhaps more miserable than ever afterwards. Yet the diffusion of Christianity proceeded with unabated force.

The uncivilised or half-civilised German tribes conquered the Empire, divided it and established new feudal kingdoms in its stead, whose laws, customs and economics were widely different from those of the Ancient World. The diffusion of the new religion, however, continued unimpaired.

It spread in times of peace and opulence as well as in centuries of war, misery and decay; it spread in periods of high civilisation, among a refined and sceptical aristocracy, as well as among rude peasants and slaves. It was disseminated by preaching and writing, by the flames of martyrdom, by secret propaganda from door to door and from mouth to mouth. It spread among the barbarians, now owing to the zeal of fearless and fanatical preachers — as among the Anglo-Saxons and in Germany at the time of Boniface — and now because a barbarian king adopted it for political reasons or out of admiration of Roman superiority, and his whole tribe followed his example — as in the case of Clovis, King of the Franks. At other times it was imposed upon an entire people by force of arms, as on the Saxons in the ninth century by Charlemagne, and on the Wends in the twelfth century by King Waldemar of Denmark and Bishop Absalon of Roeskilde.

The Christian religion spread in times of highly developed economic systems — for the period of its origin was one of large estates, great industry and a complicated financial system, a period which may well be called one of capitalism — and it spread in times of natural economy among savage warriors and rude peasants.

If, therefore, the mode of production were indeed to be considered as the real basis determining the whole " superstructure " and religion as a part of the super-structure, we should be forced to conclude, on the one hand, that the most different modes of production cause exactly the same spiritual movements and, on the other hand, that the same mode of production gives origin to the most different institutions and opinions. We might ask what strange causes these are whose effects are so uncertain and incalculable ? Or should we rather not say that there obviously exists no inter-dependency of cause and effect between the conditions of production and religion, and that those who asserted its existence, did so regardless of logic as well as of history ? For so much is clear : either a historical movement of such importance as the diffusion of Christianity was altogether independent of the economic system and had nothing whatever to do with it, or if economics had any influence upon it, this influence was modified and counter-balanced by others to such an extent as to make its effect on the movement appear insignificant.[1]

Marx says : " The social, political and intellectual

---

[1] In the light of these facts Marx's utterance on the Christian faith in *Capital*, vol. i. p. 85, seems equally rash and extravagant. He says : " Chris-tianity, treating man as an abstract being, is indeed the religion befitting the bourgeois society that lives on producing saleable goods ".

Marx might have said that the comprehension and interpretation of Christianity is different in different times and states of civilisation, and that religious practice will always become more or less adapted to the social and intellectual status of the people who have accepted its dogmas. It is, on the other hand, equally certain that the social and intellectual status of a people is deeply influenced and modified by religion.

life of a society depends on the mode of production, that is, on the entire complex of the existing conditions of production ".

We shall once more ask : What is the origin of the conditions of production, their remote or proximate cause ? Marx and those who believe in his theory, will answer : the conditions of production correspond to a certain stage of the development of the productive forces. We have, however, seen that this is a misapprehension. That the conditions of production correspond to the development of the productive forces, is true only in so far as both are inter-dependent ; and it would be equally true to say that the productive forces correspond to a certain development of the conditions of production. Neither of the two sentences contains the whole truth, and the terms used in them are vague and ambiguous. We have further seen that the productive forces are not the primary agency on which everything else depends. The primary causes of history are still undiscovered, and the only possible way to their discovery, provided that they can be known, is the most exact analysis of facts and events, and not arbitrary and hazardous generalisations.

Without pursuing this question any further here, we shall concentrate our attention upon our immediate problem, the relations between the conditions of production and the ideological superstructure. Is the proposition acceptable that, given a certain mode of production, all other social and intellectual phenomena in the same society invariably result from it ?

Cunow, intending to prove and to illustrate the truth of Marx's doctrine,[1] informs us that the economic con-

---

[1] Cf. *op. cit.* vol. ii. ch. vi., " Die Marx'sche Geschichtstheorie ".

ditions in a society assume, in the first place, a certain legal character. Now, this is true in some cases, and not in others; it is by no means always the economic conditions that determine the laws. When a warrior nation or a warrior caste subjugates a working or trading population, deprives it of the produce of its work and reduces it to mere tenancy, vassaldom or serfdom, it is not economics which determine the laws and the legal status of persons and property, but the laws and the legal status created by sheer force which determine new economic conditions.

We have repeatedly taken opportunity to indicate the deplorable vagueness and indistinctness of Marxist terminology. When a barbarous German tribe conquered a Roman province, dispossessed the landowners of the soil, yet forced them to go on cultivating it for their new lords' benefit, we cannot call the new order a new mode of production, because the mode of production is exactly the same as before, whereas the conditions of production are fundamentally changed. In Marxist literature the two terms are regularly employed as synonymous. Now, according to Marx's theory, the new conditions of production should have been brought about by some new productive force. Are we to understand that this was the brutal force of the ancient Germans? Certainly, this force, by destroying valuable goods and artistic treasures by the million, effected a fundamental change of the conditions of production in the civilised countries of antiquity, but it does not, on this account, seem advisable to call it a productive force.

From whatsoever point of view we may examine the theory of Marx, it does not prove conformable with reality.

Nobody will deny that civil as well as penal law, be it in primitive or in civilised times, is largely framed for the purpose of protecting existing economic conditions, as expressed in rights of property and of succession, in contracts and obligations. It is, however, just as undeniable that many, and not the least important, laws derive their origin from sexual or religious motives, or from motives of personal fear, from the need of the individual to be protected from physical violence and moral constraint. Now all these considerations are in no immediate, and often not even in a distant, connection with economic matters. It is further undeniable that many considerations of a non-economic nature did, in many cases, influence laws and customs in the economic sphere. We need only mention mediaeval laws against interest and usury, a good many matrimonial laws, large sections of canonical law, and many other instances.

We shall, however, admit that, law and order being a condition required for the existence of society, they belong, in a broad interpretation of the term, to the conditions of what Engels called the " production and reproduction of material life ". But that does not imply that his and Marx's theory accounts in any way for the various legal systems in force in different ages and among different nations.

Much less does it explain their religions and philosophies, their arts and sciences, in short, what is termed by Marx the ideological superstructure.

We did not need Marx's theory to tell us that the intellectual life of a period is to a large extent determined by the prevailing conditions, including economic conditions ; we knew that anything that is of importance in men's lives will occupy their thoughts and their imaginations, and that environment influences their opinions. It stands to reason and needs no explanation that an untravelled Englishman does not share the habits and opinions of an Indian, nor a Malay those of a Greenlander. These are truisms.

The question raised by Marx is whether the environment, the *milieu*, and the conditions of production in particular, exert such an exclusive influence on the entire social and intellectual life of the different strata as well as of the single individuals of any society that, given the environment, their intellectual life is bound to take a predetermined form and must go on developing in a predetermined manner ? Or are there other factors to influence and to determine it ? And, secondly, is it possible to prove Marx's thesis by pursuing an unbroken chain of causes and effects from the economic basis up to the simplest and most trivial as well as to the most extraordinary occurrences ?

Cunow's answer to these questions and his arguments on the subject are meretricious. The Materialist Conception of History, he says, does not derive men's ideology in a direct line from economic conditions, he even admits that it would be impossible to explain religion, morals and art by economics without looking for some intermediate links ; but, he adds, " the economic activity of society, being itself a whole, namely, the comprehensive integration and compensation of the single economic functions, determines the intellectual life of society as a whole, but not every single thought. The many different aggregates of thoughts which we distinguish as political, philosophical, juristic, religious, aesthetic, artistic or literary, nevertheless form a whole and influence one another. Yet, if one pursues these reciprocal concatenations to their final elements, we shall find that in every period, the social system of economy is the solid basis of the whole intellectual structure."

A worse instance of evasion and sophistry can scarcely be imagined.

The first of these three sentences is the one to be demonstrated. In the second, Cunow says that when we regard the intellectual life of a nation or of a period as a whole, it will appear to us as a whole, and he adds that the different spheres of thought exert a certain influence on one another, which is possible.[1] In the third sentence, he says that if one investigates the concatenation of causes and effects to the final link, one will find that the first sentence is true.

If one investigates the concatenation to the final link! That is what Cunow should have done and what neither he nor any other sociologist has ever attempted to do. No man has ever attempted to analyse, link for link, the connection of facts and events, nor can anybody attempt it. The reason is that it would far surpass the power of human intelligence to make out and grasp the millions and millions of facts and thoughts which form the causal chain; a good many of them would have to be traced back to past generations and remote ages; the complication of motives founded on interests, experience or feelings and nervous complexes, would be inextricable. It would be an impossible task in regard to the present, and as for the past, it would be

---

[1] Applied to the complicated intellectual life of a modern nation, the sentence does not hold good. There are in a civilised country spheres of thought which do not in any way influence each other. What influence could the religious ideas of the nonconformist communities in England have on the mathematical and experimental work of engineers all over the country, and the reverse? Yet both are important sections of English intellectual life.

impossible to arrive at even a bare knowledge of the facts.

Friedrich Engels says in one of his letters : " According to the Materialist Conception of History, the production and reproduction of material life is the fact which, in the last resort, determines everything in history. That is all that Marx and I ever affirmed." [1] The words " production and reproduction of material life ", ill-chosen as they are, cannot mean anything other than all that is necessary to ensure the preservation of mankind, and here we have once more the usual confusion of cause and condition. Procreation and self-preservation are conditions of life, but that does not imply that they determine all other conditions, unless it be by the mysterious effects of hereditary tendencies or the chemical effects of nutrition, an interpretation that is expressly excluded by Engels himself in his treatise on Feuerbach.[2] In the same letter, Engels annotates his words by adding : " If anybody distorts our meaning by asserting that the economic facts are the sole determining cause in life, he perverts our thesis into an empty, abstract and absurd phrase. The economic situation is the *basis*, but the varied elements of the superstructure — constitutions, legal forms and, above all, the reflexes of the real struggle in men's brains, that is, the political, juridical and philosophical theories — are not without influence on the

[1] Letter to Joseph Bloch, September 21, 1890. Engels' letters are quoted and partially published in various works. A collection of them appeared in the *Dokumente des Sozialismus*, ed. Ed. Bernstein, Berlin, 1901 *sqq*. As, however, the second volume, which contains the letters, is missing in the copy of the *Dokumente* in the library of the London School of Economics — which seems the only copy to be found in England — we must content ourselves with quoting the dates.

[2] *Ludwig Feuerbach und der Ausgang der klassischen Philosophie*, Litt. Nachlass (Stuttgart, 1902), p. 43.

development of the struggles that fill the annals of history; it is they which, in many cases to an overwhelming degree, determine the form which these struggles take. It is the reciprocal action of all these elements, but it is the economic movement, which, being of necessity, finally forces its way through this infinite multitude of fortuitous occurrences, that is, things and events whose connection with each other is either so superficial or so undemonstrable that we are at liberty to consider them as non-existent and negligible."

If this long-winded and confused sentence has any rational meaning, it means, in the first place, that the economic situation is indeed the basis of all, whereas constitutions and institutions as well as the theories and thoughts of men are but a superstructure; secondly, that the elements constituting the superstructure have a certain limited influence, particularly on the form which the economic struggles take; thirdly, that there exists a reciprocal action of all those elements, with the result that the economic movement " being of necessity " is the one which always carries the day, and finally, that the infinite number of events, occurrences, facts, persons and things of which life and, therefore, history consist, may be neglected whenever their connection with the economic basis cannot be demonstrated.

When we analyse these sentences, we find that Engels' indignation against those who distort his and Marx's theory is without foundation; at bottom he is himself of their opinion; the concession which he makes in this and some other passages of his letters, is only apparent. He cannot but admit that men's thoughts and theories have some effect on their actions and on the course of

events, though he regards them as mere illusions, reflexes
in their brains. He admits that they influence the outward form of the struggles and conflicts in history,
which at bottom are all of an economic nature;
the form, political, religious or national or whatsoever
else it may be, being but an illusion. In former ages,
says Engels in his treatise on Feuerbach, "when men's
souls were filled with religious ideas, their social interests
had to be placed before their minds in a religious disguise". It makes little difference whether the economic
situation is said to be the sole determining cause, or only
to override all other influences and determine the course
of history in the last resort. All these assertions are
a reflection which events produced in Marx's and Engels'
brains and which is indeed an illusion. The last sentence, however, is of a certain importance, as it contains
the confession that the infinite multitude of phenomena
of which life consists, may be neglected whenever their
connection with the economic basis cannot be seen or
demonstrated. It must be said that Engels and his
adherents made abundant use of this privilege of ignoring
facts that did not agree with their theory. The whole
passage is but a repetition of the same assertion that the
economic basis is at the bottom of all, but no proof whatever of this assertion is furnished.

Then Engels assures us in this passage that it is
" the production and reproduction of real life " that is
the primary cause determining all else; yet a few lines
farther on he says that it is the " economic movement ";
we heard before that it was the " mode of production ",
and at another time the " conditions of production "
are described as the basis of the ideological superstructure. These are four different terms; are we to assume

that they really all have exactly the same meaning ? [1] Yet as soon as anybody demands real concrete facts instead of these vague generalities, he is invariably told that he does not understand the theory. Cunow, for instance, turning against those who criticise it, affirms that by " mode of production " Marx did not mean " the activity of production in the word's proper sense " but rather the " social and material process of life as a whole ", a vague and hazy verbiage which is so comprehensive as to mean nothing in particular. A false theory finds a clear and exact terminology repugnant. Marx's meaning, however, was obviously less nebulous than Cunow would have it ; it is perfectly clear that he meant economic production in the usual sense of the word.[2]

If we allow ourselves to be guided by Marx's own words and by what Engels, Cunow, Kautsky, Labriola and others repeat in chorus, we have to accept it as their

[1] Cf. pp. 253-4.

[2] The repeated use by Marx and Engels of the words " material " and " real " was occasioned by their opposition to the idealistic philosophy of Hegel. Though we are constantly admonished not to confuse " historical " materialism with " philosophical " materialism, according to which all that is called intellectual or spiritual, is but a function or a product of what is called matter, it is to be borne in mind that the founders of historical materialism were also philosophical materialists. Expressions like " real life " or " material process of life " are directed against Hegel, who imagined that he was able to construct the whole material world, that is, the world perceived by our senses, out of abstract thought. Marx and Engels wanted to make it clear that history consists in visible and palpable facts, while the intellectual and psychic phenomena are only a by-product of the former. It will be shown that this theory is as misleading as the other.

Cunow's mode of expression, however, is incongruous and illogical, for " social and material life as a whole ", as contrasted with production alone, can only mean all observable activities and occurrences of a period, and would include a good many political, legal and other activities which according to Cunow's own doctrine belong to the superstructure. Marx certainly did not mean this.

doctrine that intellectual life, laws, institutions, morals, philosophy, science, art and religion are but a superstructure created on the conditions of production, an image in the brain, reflecting the struggles and events created by the conditions of production.

If we demand proofs, the adherents of the theory excuse themselves by alleging that proofs cannot be given, because there are too many intermediate links obscuring the concatenation, which, they assert, is nevertheless certain. That is to say, they believe in the theory but are unable to furnish scientific proofs. To hold good in science, the thesis that philosophy, art, religion, etc., are determined by the conditions of production, would have to be demonstrated, not in one or two, or even in twenty, but in innumerable cases, and it would, in each case, have to be demonstrated, by proving the causal dependence, link for link, of art, philosophy, etc., upon the conditions of production. As we pointed out before, this is, of course, impossible and has, therefore, never been attempted.

We, on the contrary, were in a position to show that the Christian religion, the tenets and moral commandments of which were diametrically opposed to the creeds prevailing in antique times, maintained itself and spread under the most divergent conditions of production. When we find that the most different modes of production, those of highly civilised nations as well as those of uncivilised warrior tribes, were, for a thousand years, compatible with the same ideology, we are surely justified in concluding that the ideology of these nations was determined by some cause other than economics. And in view of the fact that the civilised Romans, as well as the half-savage Germans, Slavs and Irishmen, accepted a strange religion coming to them from a small country in the East, we are further entitled to say that the influence of the mode of production on moral and religious opinions must be comparatively small and is, above all, uncertain and incalculable. For I do not suppose that Marxist authors will assert that the mode of production or the economic basis was identical in imperial Rome, under the kings of the Franks, in savage Ireland, under the Saxon emperors and in the countries of the heathen Slavs.

Nevertheless, we are far from denying that economics may have a certain influence on religious views, especially among primitive nations, though some of the cases mentioned by Cunow are open to objection. He says, for instance, that the division of labour among men and women in the South Sea Islands at last took on a religious character. Originally adopted for economic reasons, these customs became fixed by tradition, and finally, owing to the fear of evil spirits, were made immutable as a religious formula. Now, the belief in spirits, which existed among the civilised Romans quite as much as among primitive negroes, is certainly not due to economic reasons, but to the need of finding a cause for unexplained occurrences, a purely intellectual phenomenon. The case alleged by Cunow to prove his theory seems to prove the reverse, namely, that purely economic customs are influenced by religious ideas.

It is on the nature and origin of " ideas " and of " ideal driving forces ", and the part which they fulfil in history, that the main stress is laid in the polemics for and against the materialist conception of history. And it has to be admitted that Marx's opponents often misunderstood his theory and ascribed to him and to his adherents opinions which they did not hold. They reproached Marx with denying the existence and operation of ideal driving forces in history. " On the contrary ", Cunow replied, " it is Marx's doctrine that the economic forces must first be transformed into ideal motives before they can compel men to act. These ideal forces, however, are not primary : they are but a secondary product of the economic system."

Here, again, Cunow's interpretation is manifestly inexact. Marx did not go as far as that. The direct effect of economic motives on men's thoughts and actions is so patent in the majority of cases, both in everyday life and in history, that Marx would never have said anything so palpably preposterous. Marx did not assert that economic changes actuate men solely in the shape of ideal motives. All he said was that " in a social crisis men grow conscious of the conflict between the productive forces and the conditions of production, in ideological forms ". Mr. John Strachey explains Marx's meaning well by giving the following instance : " Men think that they overthrow, say, a feudalistic monarchy for the sake of the ideal of liberty, equality and fraternity. And so they do. This is the only conscious motive in their heads, and it is absurd to deny that it is their real motive. The ' ideology ' (the general world outlook) of which the slogan ' liberty, equality and fraternity ' is the epitome, has filled their consciousness completely. It is only if we go behind this ideology that we discover that it has grown out of the conflict between changing, developing, technical and economic conditions and a static political structure." [1] We shall, in another place, examine whether

[1] John Strachey, *The Theory and Practice of Socialism*, ch. xxviii., " The Materialist Conception of History " (London, 1936), p. 362.

this description of the revolution is in accordance with facts or not ; we now quote it for the reason that it is a perfect interpretation of what Marx meant in the sentence quoted above, and what is generally meant in Marxist literature by the transformation of motives in men's brains. There are certainly many cases in which this transformation [1] of motives takes place, and it is by no means restricted to economic motives : modern science has shown that the most various transformations are taking place in men's souls ; it has also been recognised long ago that men are apt to deceive themselves as to the motives of their actions. It is the psychologist's and the historian's task to distinguish between these cases in which men's motives are clear and patent and they themselves are aware of what is impelling them to act, and those in which an unconscious transformation of motives has taken place, and, in the latter, to discriminate between men's true motives and those which are only apparent. He who thinks he can tabulate the infinite variations of reality and explain every event in accordance with the same formula, is sure to find himself on the wrong scent.

At the time when Marx wrote his propositions, he and Engels — as already observed — joined issue with Hegel. It was against his conception of history that their polemics were intended in the first place. Engels was right in calling Hegel's sentence that " Greek

---

[1] Transformation is of course not the right term. We must rather assume a causal relation between the true economic and the illusive ideal motive which impels men to act : just as Pareto would probably say that the " residue " (instinct) produces the " derivation " (theories, etc.) and not that it is transformed into it. Yet, as Marx, nurtured with Hegelian philosophy, speaks of a " form " in which men grow conscious of economic conflicts, we may as well employ the term " transformation ".

history is essentially an elaboration of the fine personality " an empty phrase and a mere assertion. Yet his and Marx's explanation of Greek art and culture as derived from the mode of economic production is likewise a mere assertion and no better than an empty phrase. The mode of production of a great number of nations was perfectly similar to that of the Greeks, yet none of them produced an art and a civilisation in any way comparable to theirs. In the same place, Engels says that " it is not inconsistent to believe in ideal impulses and driving forces, but it is inconsistent not to carry the investigation any further until the motive causes behind those driving forces and impulses are discovered ". That, however, is just the inconsistency with which we reproach Engels and all Marxist historians : they never attempt really to dive into the matter and to carry the investigation further until the motive causes are discovered. It is true, they assert that these last causes are already discovered, giving out that the economic facts, the forces and the conditions of production are these last causes, but this is not carrying the investigation back to these causes, being nothing more than a mere assertion. They give us, so to speak, their word of honour that it really is the case. A word of honour, however, is no scientific proof. We are not satisfied. Had they, in any real case, pursued the investigation back to the economic causes, they would be able to pursue the way in the opposite direction. If their theory was more than a mere hypothesis, they would be in a position to demonstrate how the economic conditions create the ideology, by exposing to view the causal chain, link for link.

On p. 35 *et seq.* we examined some ineffectual attempts

to do this, made by Marxist authors; and we were in a position to show that though they pretended to apply the inductive method, their conclusions were in reality mere deductions made possible by an insufficient knowledge of the historical facts.

Cunow admits, not without regret, that the question as to how this transformation of economic facts and motives into ideal driving forces is brought about, has not been treated at all by Marx, while Engels has given it only superficial attention. This is indeed to be regretted, as the acceptance or rejection of the whole theory depends upon it. What Engels said on the question is certainly very superficial. He says in a letter to Franz Mehring: " The image of a period, as reflected in man's intellect, is determined by the form of economics and by the social conditions produced by it. This reflected image forms, so to speak, a given intellectual environment, a *milieu* composed of thoughts and feelings, in which the single individual is brought up and from which he receives, according to his social position, his impressions, feelings and opinions." [1] The first part of this passage contains but another repetition of the same assertion, while in the second, Engels speaks of the effect which the general ideology of his environment has on the individual. The most important link, however, is missing; for we are not told in what manner and why the reflected image in men's brains is determined by economics. It seems that we must accept it on trust. Let us, however, examine the propositions enunciated by Engels, such as they are. There are, according to Engels, two degrees or stages of causation: the form of economics determining the general ideology which

[1] Letter to Franz Mehring of January 25, 1894.

in turn determines the feelings and opinions of the individual. We must say at once that Engels' argument seems neither well considered nor phrased with precision. The general ideology of a nation or a society or a class of society consists of views, opinions, images, etc., which do not float in the air, but exist in the brains of individuals who make up society : the general ideology has no separate existence of itself ; it does not really differ from the individual ideologies ; it is at best the sum of these ideologies. What Engels wanted to convey is that the common or similar ideologies of the greater number of the individuals composing a society or a class of this society determine those of the younger individuals growing up in this environment. Now, this is true in many cases though by no means in all, and even in those cases in which it holds good, it is only partly true.

A Marxist might object that the intellectual environment does not consist of opinions only, but of laws, institutions, policies, etc. It is true that the word *milieu* is also a rather vague term. If, however, it is to comprise institutions and conditions of all sorts, economics and production certainly belong to it, and Engels' gradation would be meaningless. Moreover, even if accepted in this larger sense, the proposition would be quite as untenable.

Cunow, quoting Engels' words and commenting on them, gives as an instance of their accuracy that the same fact will affect civilised and primitive man in a different way, and that the same impression will produce different thoughts in members of different social classes or of peoples in a different state of civilisation. He has, however, to admit that not only the ideologies of different classes, orders and professions differ from each other, but that even the individual within one and the same class or group may have a particular ideology, and he concludes by saying that the ideas and imaginations of the individual are determined not only by their objects and by the individual's environment, but also by the latter's personal capacity for perception and combination.[1] Yet Cunow is not aware that his concessions destroy his own argument, for how are economics to determine ideology by means of environment if the effect of environment is made uncertain by individual qualities ?

We do indeed find that the opinions of men belonging to the same class, and brought up under exactly the same conditions, are nevertheless quite different. How is it that from the same class of the Roman Optimates there arose men like Scipio and Opimius who advocated aristocratic rule and interest, and men like the Gracchi ? That in the French nobility of the Ancien Régime we find conservative, liberal and revolutionary members ? How is it — the question has often been put — that the founders of Socialism and the leaders of the modern labour movement have for long years come almost without exception from the bourgeoisie, that is, from an environment which, if there were any truth in the theory, would necessarily have implanted in them directly opposite views ? We may even go still further and find the influence of environment still more questionable, seeing that men procreated by the same parents, brought up in the same house and educated by the same teachers, nevertheless develop widely differing views and opinions.

If anybody should say that these are but exceptions, we should reply that where there are exceptions, there

[1] Cunow, *op. cit.* vol. ii. p. 220.

is no law in the scientific sense of the word, least of all when the exceptions are so frequent as to be noticeable everywhere and every day. We shall see, too, that it is these exceptions which are of the greatest, and even of the only real, importance in the evolution of mankind. If environment did determine their ideology, all men living in the same environment would necessarily have the same ideas and pursue the same ends. It would be impossible that from the same class, the same set and even the same family, there should arise, by the side of brothers and sisters who follow the common track, some original and revolutionary thinker. Either environment determines ideology or does not determine it, but an environment that in some cases determines men's ideology and in other cases fails to do so, is either no causal factor at all, or else there must needs exist other factors which suspend or counteract its effects in numerous cases. If there are exceptions there must be a cause that accounts for them. We know that these exceptions are in part determined by innate qualities of the individual, and in part by special and purely personal impressions and experiences during the individual's lifetime. Of these the first, belonging to the enigmatic phenomena of heredity, are up to this time hidden from our knowledge, while the latter are but rarely discernible other than to the individual experiencing them. It was thought for some time that the individual is the result of two elements: heredity and environment. It has been rightly said that this is trying to explain an unknown value by means of two still less known. For heredity, especially as far as the transmission of the subtle qualities of the intellect is concerned, is an unexplored field of which we know next to nothing. And the environment, the *milieu* of a person, consists of such an enormous and incalculable mass of facts, events and impressions as to be quite beyond the range of our insight and knowledge. In no single case is it possible for us really to determine it. That man is influenced by his environment is not to be doubted. But we are quite unable to tell in what way he is influenced by it, nor can we know which, of the countless component parts of a man's environment, will exercise or has exercised a decisive influence. There are, no doubt, cases in which we are able to state such influences *ex post* when the effects are clearly seen, but even then we can do so, as a rule, only in rough outlines and with no real certainty. The influence of the environment on the individual depends, besides, to a great extent on the latter's personality, different individuals being very differently impressed and influenced by the same facts. Some individuals react with great force to certain impressions while others exposed to the same conditions do not react at all. There are persons who, though grown up in the country and living surrounded by natural scenery, yet derive no pleasure from it. Some of the persons bred up amidst books and by scholars will grow up to be scholars themselves, whereas others will develop an aversion to science and books. There are people without any artistic taste or inclination who passed their childhood in houses decorated with consummate art, whereas the same environment will imbue others with an eternal longing for beautiful surroundings. In the same way, there are persons in whom the conditions of production will create opinions answering to their economic interest, or what they believe to be their economic interest, while the same conditions of production will induce in others

78

the opposite opinions, based on their moral sense. Possibly the latter will indignantly demand that the existing conditions of production be changed : they may start a propaganda to this end and create an intellectual and political movement. Their moral indignation is perhaps to be traced back to obscure hereditary influences, to certain impressions made on their forefathers in a remote past. It may be so, but we have not the slightest proof of it, and we are not entitled to draw conclusions from uncertain suppositions and unauthenticated beliefs, or if we do so, our conclusions will be void of any scientific value.

Thus, socialistic or revolutionary ideas sprang up in the heads of men belonging to the aristocracy or the middle classes.

To this a Marxist might make the following objection : History, he would say, is an uninterrupted struggle of classes, fought out in ideological forms. The reasons and arguments which men allege in fighting it out, are but the ideal forms in which this struggle appeals to their consciousness. " New ideas will spring up in the heads of that part of the population that is affected by a change in the conditions of production : they are, so to speak, an ideological precipitate of the conditions of production." [1] Among the Roman proletarians dispossessed of their native soil, or among the workmen defrauded of the surplus value produced by the work of their hands, discontent spreads and an effervescent state of mind, and at the same time, in the heads of intelligent and educated persons like the Gracchi in ancient Rome, or Marx and Engels in our time, new ideas will germinate and plans of reform. The effervescence in the heads

[1] Cunow, *op. cit.* vol. ii. p. 220.

of the proletarians and the new programmes in those of the leaders are both reflections created in men's brains by the conditions of production. If economic conditions were not in a bad state, there would neither be an effervescence in the class affected by them, nor would new ideas be born and take shape in men's brains.[1]

We shall admit the truth of this argument in that particular case. Obviously, feelings and new ideas concerning the conditions of production could not well have come into existence unless the state of these conditions had called them forth. It is, however, noteworthy, that even in this case the new ideas did not arise from among the class affected by the change but, on the contrary, from that part of the population which was not, or certainly much less, affected or even profited by it.[2] And if our opponent should reply: All strata of a population are affected by a change in the conditions of production, all Romans felt the disastrous conse-

---

[1] In a passage of the " *Communist Manifesto* " it is said : " At the moment when the struggle between the classes draws near the decisive stage, a portion of the ruling class detaches itself from it and joins the revolutionary class, which represents the future. Just as in former days a section of the nobility took the side of the bourgeoisie, so to-day a section of the bourgeoisie makes common cause with the Proletariat, in particular that section of the ideologists among the bourgeois who are capable of understanding theoretically the entire historical movement." This is perfectly true ; it happens even long before the struggle reaches its decisive stage. But it is something widely different from what is stated above. We are not speaking of those members of the ruling class who join the revolutionary movement at a later stage but of those who came before it, who were its founders and leaders, and who in modern times established its theory.

[2] Marx and Engels could, in 1845, " consider only themselves properly as members of the Communist party, and, maybe, a small number of intellectuals, but there were no workmen to back them up ". " The proletarians knew very little of their persons and still less of their writings " Gustav Mayer, *Friedrich Engels : Eine Biographie* (Berlin, 1920), and 1933, vol. i. pp. 252, 260.

quences of the changed mode of production in the last two centuries of the Republic, the exploitation of the conquered nations, the large estates and the usurious practices of the Optimates, the misery of the masses, one part of the population having grown immoderately rich and the other intolerably poor, the whole social system was put out of gear, the new ideas were bound to come ; in what heads they first arose depended on the necessary degree of intelligence.

All right, we should say, this proves only what an important part is played in all historical movements and changes by personal gifts and by intelligence. Moreover, the Romans themselves knew perfectly well that everybody is affected by great economic changes. They knew from experience that discontented masses are apt to be riotous and that, whenever this happened, persons were found who proposed some plan for redress, plans which, in some cases, led to important consequences and in others proved abortive. And all educated persons in the nineteenth century knew as much as this. We did not need Marx and Engels to tell us. Marx and Engels, however, enunciated a doctrine different from this hackneyed wisdom, they asserted that all opinions and ideologies are *determined* by the conditions of production, which is to say that given conditions of production will of necessity produce a certain corresponding ideology. But neither Marx nor Engels nor any of their followers was ever able to demonstrate that this is really the case. The episodes from Roman and from our own history which he quotes as cases in point, prove, like the instances given before, that the same conditions of production are liable to produce quite different ideologies in different minds. Nor could any of these writers ever explain why and how this influence of economic production on men's ideologies takes effect. We saw that Engels tried to resolve the problem by declaring that the effect is reached by the intermediate action of environment, and we have shown how unsound and incongruous his reasoning is.

Other followers of the theory thought to find the key to the entire process in the interpolation of interest. As Engels interpolated environment, they interpolated interest. This seems, at first sight, to be a much more plausible theory, as there cannot be the slightest doubt that people are constantly actuated by their interests. It does not seem illogical to say : men's economic activities give rise to countless interests, men are actuated by their economic interests to such a degree that not only are the great majority of their actions directed towards the promotion of these interests, but their very opinions are constantly influenced by them ; they approve whatever serves their interests and condemn whatever runs counter to them ; and in a great many cases they are not even aware that their opinions and views have been determined — unconsciously — by their interest.

All this is perfectly true. It is so obviously true that many people are of the erroneous opinion that this is the meaning of the Materialist Conception of History : that men are actuated only by material, that is, by economic interests, yet this is by no means the case. Marx, says Cunow, " did not call his conception of history ' materialist ' because he thought men are prompted by material motives only, but because the material process of life of a society is the basis of its intellectual life. The Marxists do not deny the existence of ideal interests ; what they say is, that all interests, ideal and material, collective and individual, are determined by the conditions of production. " Interest ", Cunow adds, " is an intermediate factor by means of which the economic system exerts its determining influence on ideology ; it is, however, a factor the co-operation of which is not absolutely necessary. Even without its co-operation, a certain social environment is apt to create certain ideas." This is one of the usual vague and arbitrary assertions and untenable generalisations, by means of which Marxist authors make short work of a difficulty.

All these gradations, these suppositions of intermediate links, are perfectly fortuitous. Sometimes the development actually proceeds in this manner, whereas in other cases it takes a different or even the opposite course. Men's interests determine economics quite as much or even more than they are determined by economics. The alleged intermediate factors, interest or environment, sometimes take effect, producing certain ideas, whereas in other cases they have not the slightest influence upon a person. Even though, in the examples just given, we selected cases in which men's ideology was concerned with, and indeed took its origin from the conditions of production of the time, we had to state that the connection was merely fortuitous, and that even in events of this kind — the agrarian troubles in ancient Rome or the social problem of our own time — in which the economic character of the causes is evident, their effect is uncertain and indeterminate.

At the time of the Reformation, in the long wars between Catholics and Protestants, men were moved alternately or even simultaneously by religious dissensions, rivalry for power and by economic or personal

83

interests, motives that sometimes clashed and sometimes co-operated.

To understand such a period, a close and cautious investigation of numerous individual cases is indispensable. To the follower of the Marxist theory, however, it is a simple matter, doubts do not assail him and all questions are answered in advance. The Reformation in Germany, says Labriola, was an economic uprising of the German nation against the exploitation of the Papal Court.[1] Luther erroneously mistook the movement in his favour for a return to true Christianity. " When we consider the consequences visible only long afterwards, the growth of the territorial sovereignty of the princes at the expense of the Emperor's power and of the international influence of the Pope, the growing power of the towns as contrasted with the feudal lords, the suppression of the peasant rising, and of the truly proletarian movement of the Anabaptists, when we consider all this, we are in a position to reconstruct the economic causes of the Reformation. In the same proportion as the Reformation progresses, these consequences are revealed. This is an obvious proof. . . ." " The profane and prosaic driving forces behind the Reformation are particularly manifest in France, where the movement was not successful, in the Netherlands, where the conflicting economic interests are clearly visible, beside the national antagonism, in the struggle against the Spaniards, and still more so in England, where the religious reform was carried through by brute force, so that the transition to a state of things preparing the necessary conditions of capitalism and modern bourgeois-domination is evident."

[1] *La Conception matérialiste de l'histoire*, p. 116.

Labriola is strangely mistaken in the chronology of events. The struggle of the princes against the Emperor had been going on for five hundred years before the Reformation. The power of the cities as contrasted with that of the feudal lords had been constantly growing during three hundred years, and for four hundred years already all the nations of Europe had complained of being exploited by the Papal Court; an English chronicler of the thirteenth century wrote that Pope Gregory IX's encyclical letter against the Emperor Frederick II in 1239 " would have roused all the world against the Emperor, but that the Romish Court exacted so much money from all parts of the world ".

The amount of the taxes paid in England to the Pope was five times in excess of the taxes paid to the King. The causes which Labriola believes to have produced the Reformation had been operating for nearly five hundred years without leading to it; which is to say that the economic and political conditions had, as far as Church and State were concerned, been the same for centuries, but the ideology in the past centuries had been different. Many people had been indignant or critical; there had repeatedly been reformatory efforts within the Church; but those who had seriously risen against her, like Petrus Waldus, John Wycliffe, Huss and their adherents, remained hopeless minorities, which were sooner or later defeated by the Church backed by the overwhelming majority of the population of Europe.

Labriola's interpretation of the Reformation has all the defects of a *prima facie* conclusion. A closer investigation of the period would have shown him that, whereas the religious movement in the single countries of Europe was more or less the same, the political and economic development was different in each. The mere fact that the Catholic Flemings, despite national and economic interests, remained loyal to the Spanish Crown, should have made Labriola think twice.

His strangest and most objectionable argument, however, is that, from unforeseen consequences, realised long afterwards, of an event or a movement, it should be possible to reconstruct its causes. If it is inadmissible, from the mere fact that of two events one succeeded the other, to conclude that the second was caused by the first, it is still less admissible to infer the causes of a movement from its eventual consequences. Yet this is a paralogism habitual to Marxist historians. We might as well conclude that, because a spark from a locomotive kindled a forest, the train was despatched for this end, or, to remain in the sphere of history, that because by Alexander's conquests the Greek language spread over the near East, a circumstance which contributed, three centuries later, to the rapid expansion of the Christian religion, this was the true cause of Alexander's expeditions. Mediaeval thinkers used to draw similar conclusions.

Marx himself condemned this mode of reasoning. " It is a distorting speculation ", said he, " to declare a later historical development to have been the cause of a precedent event or development. What is designated by the words ' destination ', ' purpose ', ' root ', ' idea ' is only an abstraction from later history, an abstraction from the influence which former events had on a later development." [1]

We willingly admit that in nearly all cases economic interests and economic conflicts supervened upon the

[1] *Deutsche Ideologie*, p. 34.

religious dissensions, co-operating or interfering with them. The conduct of the princes and governments who took part in the wars of religion, was directed, in a large measure, by worldly aims. But the religious movement was primary, the princes and governments profited by the situation created by it. Many princes, moreover, were sincerely religious; King Gustavus Adolphus, for instance, was as anxious to promote the Protestant religion as to aggrandise Swedish power and influence. To understand any event, any movement in life or history, it is first necessary exactly to retrace its origin and development. How did the Reformation come to pass ? Some individual, or several, priests or laymen, rose and preached from sincere conviction what they thought was the true faith, needful for men's salvation. Some other individuals, many perhaps, convinced and won over by their words, joined them and helped to propagate their doctrine. Others, just as naturally, were shocked by it. They, and especially the established Church, feeling its power and its very existence threatened, turned against the preachers and their flock and prevailed upon the authorities to forbid the movement and take severe measures against the agitators. The persecuted, looking out for protection, addressed themselves quite naturally to powerful persons whom they knew to be in favour of the new doctrine. Very often, and probably in the great majority of cases, the protectors were perfectly sincere and filled with true religious zeal. Soon, however, the opportunity of laying hold of the patrimony and of increasing their own power enticed them. It is not in man's nature to refuse great advantages which are within his reach. Thus different motives are combined and often confused by the acting persons, and the movement is no longer purely religious ; political and economic objects, pursued by its leaders as well as the afflux of lukewarm and adventurous camp-followers, alter its nature.

Now, instead of carefully scrutinising and examining the course which things are apt to take, the Marxists have their conclusion ready to hand ; they know before-hand that every movement must have an economic cause ; their judgment is biassed and their method purely deductive : they do not study the movement in order to find its cause, but look for an economic cause that may possibly suit this particular movement. So, in the case of the Reformation, they take the tributary that has polluted the river and made its course deviate, to be the original source.

There are, however, movements and events in great number which have no connection whatever with pro-duction and economy. During the third and fourth centuries of the Christian era the Church was divided into sects, which fought each other with deadly hate and fury. They called themselves Orthodox and Donatists, Arians, Semiarians and, when the division, founded on the most hair-splitting interpretations, went still deeper in later years, they were called Homoousians, Homoe-ousians, Homoeans and Anomoeans. These sects had adherents in all parts of the population, the court itself was divided, millions and millions of persons grew excited about them ; many thousands lost their lives and enormous quantities of economic goods were de-stroyed in endless conflicts and brawls. A new idea on a mystery, crossing some monk's or bishop's brain, a differing opinion on the interpretation of some passage in the Bible, sufficed to produce bloodshed and civil war.

Abstruse religious thoughts not only lived on for centuries, but exerted a powerful influence and left bloodstained traces in the history of the Church. All these people, belonging to the different sects and fighting for them, lived under exactly the same conditions of production ; the material interest of their leaders would have required their giving up their differences and seeking a reconciliation, which the emperors, on whose favour they absolutely depended, admonished them to do in ever repeated rescripts. The monarchs implored their subjects, and the clergy in particular, not to endanger the Christian faith and doctrine for the sake of small and unimportant discrepancies ; they exhorted and requested them rather to unite against their common enemies, the pagans, who exulted in their discord and derided their nonsensical disputations. No doubt, questions of personal authority and influence played a part in the struggle, especially in the later dispute on the two natures of Christ, which distracted the nations in the sixth century ; but surely less than the furious wish of leaders and followers to see their own opinion triumphant and force the others to adopt it. And however personal ambitions may have inflamed the discord and exasperated it, this does not change the fact that shades of opinions, phenomena of a purely intellectual nature, lived their own life and nearly proved capable of destroying a society and its economic system.

Let us consider another case. If there ever was a scientific discovery whose consequences shook the world, it was that of the Canon of Frauenburg, Nicolas Copernicus, who established the truth of the earth revolving round the sun. It took him some fifteen years of intricate calculations to substantiate it. Now, in what connection these calculations stood to the mode of production in the sixteenth century we should be curious to know. We shall admit that a certain development of economic conditions is required to make scientific research possible. It is obvious that, in a primitive state of agriculture or nomadic life, the intellectual faculties of individuals are not sufficiently differentiated to enable a number of them to devote themselves to scientific studies, and, moreover, centuries of continual scientific application have to pass before men are likely to become capable of such subtle and difficult calculations. Admitting this, we do not imply that the economic changes are the basic fact in this development.[1] We know that in the early Middle Ages, at a time when economic production was primitive enough, once the Franks had outgrown their first barbaric state and acquired a varnish of Roman culture, science and a subtle philosophy was cultivated under the Carolingian emperors. We may even go so far as to admit that without the economic development of modern times, those comprehensive studies and investigations in every domain of human thought and experience which constitute modern science, would have been impossible. It is, however, obvious, from the very nature of the human mind, that, once begun, scientific discoveries had to be continued and

[1] To make the calculations of Copernicus possible, a development of mathematical science was necessary which took the following course: the Arabs, having learned geometry from the Greeks and algebra from the Hindus, developed both branches and, moreover, found a new kind of trigonometry. Their science as well as the numerals which they had also borrowed from India, were introduced into Europe at the time of the Crusades and led to the invention of decimal fractions. These purely intellectual developments made possible in their concatenation the discovery of the true nature of the solar system. Yet, the birth of the individual Nicolas Copernicus in the year 1473, and his qualification to carry out the work, remains an unexplained and inexplicable phenomenon.

developed. One observation, one experience succeeded the other, every conclusion led to new and farther-reaching conclusions and ever new hypotheses supplanted those which had preceded them. Economic conditions might give the opportunities necessary for scientific research or make it possible ; yet, once it had set in, they no longer had the slightest influence, either on the results of the scientist's observations or on his logical deductions. That is why Marx and Engels' exclamation : " Where would natural science be without commerce and industry ? "[1] misses the mark. We might as well cry — where would the hunter be without the game, the tiller without a field ? Yet, for all that, it was not the game that invented hunting, nor the field that discovered plough, manure and seed, but men's brains that were necessary to accomplish this. The influence of economics may induce men to give particular attention to certain provinces of scientific research, because the discoveries in this individual branch of science are of importance for production, yet even in these cases it is production that is furthered by the discoveries, rather than the reverse. And, above all, economics and economic interests can never determine the results of investigation. This is most important ; for the entire economic development is dependent on these results on which it has no influence whatever.[2] It is, as pointed out before, a

[1] *Deutsche Ideologie*, p. 33.

[2] " It is not the discoveries or the inventions which produce social revolutions, but the social revolutions which produce the discoveries." Mehring, *op. cit.* p. 455.

No doubt. First was great industry, then came the invention of the steam-engine and of the dynamos ; first came the great change in the system of communications and transport, and then followed the invention of the railway and the steamship. The logic of these writers is on a level with their knowledge.

constant logical mistake of Marxist thinkers that they are unable to distinguish between opportunity, conditions, etc., on one side and determining causes on the other.

It is, however, by no means the only mistake. Engels says in one of his letters : " The thinker imagines driving forces that are either false or only apparent. Treating an intellectual process, he is apt to derive its form from thought alone, either from his own or that of his predecessors. He investigates thought alone, believing without misgivings that it was in its turn produced by mere thought and not suspecting for a moment that it may be connected with some more distant process independent of thought. . . . Luther and Calvin defeating the official Catholic Church, Hegel mastering Kant and Fichte, Rousseau superseding by his *Contrat social* constitutional Montesquieu, appear to them as phenomena within the sphere of theology, philosophy or political science, as a stage in the history of these sciences having no relation whatever to other developments beyond their sphere. And since in the present middle class the illusion has become dominant that the capitalist system of production is eternal and the last stage of economics, even the fact that the physiocrats and Adam Smith prevailed over the mercantilist school of economists is regarded as a victory of mere thought, not as a reflection in thought of changed economic conditions, but as a final attainment of insight into conditions that existed from the beginning and everywhere." [1]

It is no doubt true that authors who wrote the history of some particular branch of science neglected, in many cases, to trace the connection between the development

[1] Letter to Franz Mehring of July 14, 1889.

of this science and the development of mankind and society in other respects. It is possible that some of them were unaware of the inter-connection of things ; most of them, however, were probably of opinion that their task was merely to describe the changes and the progress in that particular sphere. Engels, while aware of these inter-connections and mutual inter-dependencies of the phenomena of human evolution, errs in his turn by ascribing an exaggerated importance and influence to one single group of these phenomena, by misjudging the nature of this inter-dependence in general, and by failing to see the momentous differences in the measure and degree in which mental phenomena may be influenced by economic and political changes.

A conception of history, a moral or philosophical system, certain ideas concerning laws and institutions may to a certain extent be influenced by the conditions of production or by politics ; it is very possible and even probable that they will change when the political or economic system changes. Exact science, however, remains unaffected. Scientists may be killed or exiled, laboratories destroyed and science decay and perish in a return to barbarism, but its results and its theories remain unchanged. From the multiplication tables to the infinitesimal calculus, mathematical propositions remain the same through all ages as long as the human mind remains the same. What Oswald Spengler said to the contrary has long been proved false.[1] Animals, plants, the strata of the earth, chemical and physical phenomena, are not affected by changes in the world of man, and therefore neither the conditions of production

[1] Cf. Hessenberg Gerhard, professor of mathematics at the University of Breslau, *Vom Sinn der Zahlen* (Leipzig, 1822).

nor the will of a dictator have any influence on zoology, botany, geology, chemistry, etc. Since scientists have ceased to be led astray by their imagination and begun serious research, they are bound to state what is in nature, just as a true historian is bound to state what he finds in sources and documents. He may misinterpret them, he may even state an untruth ; but black does not turn white because a man declares or a government decrees that it should be so.

Now, it is precisely these discoveries that are not dependent on social changes, which have, in their turn, influenced the opinions, the philosophy, the religion, in short, the whole ideology of our time to an extreme degree ; they have shaken ancient ideological systems to their very foundations and have caused new systems to arise in their place. The fundamental basis of these new ideologies is autonomous and exempt from all influence on the part of the conditions of production.[1]

A discussion took place in the beginning of this century between different Marxist authors on the question whether the so-called " ideal factors " were capable of living a life of their own and of " following their own laws ", or whether they were at all times strictly dependent on the conditions of production of the period. Several of these writers, as, for instance, Edward Bernstein, Alfred Braunthal and Max Adler, took the part of intellect, ready to concede it a certain independence. Kautsky and others, especially Cunow, pounced upon

[1] A certain Mr. F. Tischler, struck by this manifest independence of science, tried to save the situation by declaring in an article, " The Materialist Conception of History and Natural Science ", that natural science did not form a part of the superstructure, but rather of the foundation. It quite escaped him that, as soon as this is accepted, the whole theory founders. *Neue Zeit* of February 24, 1906, p. 223.

this shocking heresy. The heretics — nearly all Marxist literature is of a dogmatic or exegetic character — had discovered some texts in the works of Engels which they thought justified their opinions. As if any text were needed to justify them ! To anybody who is not blinded and prejudiced by a dogma, life and history offer the millionfold proof that thoughts, beliefs, theories, even the merest nonsense, are capable of living a life of their own, not to mention works of art and scientific theories and discoveries which, like religion, have often outlived races, civilisations and the most widely differing social systems. Labriola, while denying that intellectual currents or creations of the intellect can exist independent of economic conditions, adds in the same breath that " owing to inherited opinions the origin of which may be traced back to prehistoric times, and to men's habitual submissiveness, antiquated tendencies in art and religion are apt obstinately to maintain themselves ", which is to say he admits independence, calling it obstinacy. Moreover, Labriola informs us in the same passage that we are indebted to the Babylonians for the dial of our clocks and to the Arabs for algebra, proving by his very words that thoughts may have an existence independent of the society, or form of society, which gave them birth. The existence of books, which may be read five thousand years after having been first conceived and written, is a sufficient proof. People may die, races become extinct, but tradition or written documents will carry on their thoughts and deliver them to future generations, living under conditions of production that have little or nothing in common with those prevailing in such bygone times. And none can tell what influence those thoughts of a nearly forgotten society may have upon the living.

A few ancient treatises, rediscovered by chance in the eighth and ninth centuries of our era, not only determined the course of studies in schools and universities during the Middle Ages, but the trend and character of all mediaeval philosophy and, to a large extent, that of modern philosophy also. The *Isagoge* of Porphyrius, found among these manuscripts, gave rise to the endless controversy between Nominalists and Realists. A grammatical treatise having been found among them, grammar lessons have formed a part of instruction in languages to this day. The treatises discovered then and there had been composed at different times between the fourth century before and the fifth after Christ, yet they influenced the studies and the school teaching of nearly all white nations for more than a thousand years.

But how about the origin of these thoughts outliving generations and systems? There are individuals in whom the intellect of mankind manifests itself, as it were, in concentrated form. Here, Marx's theory of history is found to be hopelessly at fault. The appearance of those men who opened new outlooks to their generation or who successfully took the lead in some critical situation, is in nowise connected with, or dependent on, the conditions of production. If anybody would contend that it was owing to the development of the productive forces and to the existing conditions of production that such men as Kant and Newton, Rousseau and Mirabeau, Goethe and Napoleon were born, men whose influence extended over a great part of the earth and far into the unknown depth of time, he is bound to prove it and to demonstrate why and how the conditions of production caused the birth of these men at this particular time;

otherwise his assertion is idle talk and nothing but an arbitrary hypothesis.

We might have expected that the authors who wrote on the Materialist Conception of History, should at least have made an attempt to do this. But what they say on the subject is indeed idle talk. Cunow informs us that men of genius are influenced by their environment and by prevailing opinions, which is not to the point, being as natural as it is uninteresting. It is what is new in the man's gifts, the qualities by which he distinguishes himself from his fellow men, all that he does not owe to environment, that interests us in a man of genius. If he had no extraordinary qualities, if environment had made him exactly like all the rest, we would not call him a man of genius nor be interested in his personality. As Xénopol well said : " Les conditions peuvent faire tout excepté le génie lui-même ". Cunow adds that genius, when it is of surpassing greatness and too much in advance of its time, frequently goes unrecognised and proves ineffectual. But what does its failure prove, except that contemporaries were much less intelligent, that the difference between them and the man of genius was in this case even greater than in others ? And the fact that the work of great men often has its full effect much later neither impairs its effect nor its importance. Nothing could be more banal than the frequent objections that there are limits to the work of genius, that great men are liable to make mistakes, that their discoveries are often imperfect or are later rejected and replaced by newer ones. Nobody ever thought or said that men of genius are all-powerful or infallible.

Partly from a misconceived political interest, to ingratiate themselves with the multitude, and partly from inability to explain genius, the adherents of the Marxist theory are fond of minimising the part which genius has played in history. When they have to treat the subject, they like to speak of the " so-called great men ". Engels, for instance, in his treatise on Feuerbach, writes : " To find out the causes, the driving forces which are more or less distinctly reflected in the heads of the acting masses and their leaders, the so-called great men, so as to become their conscious motives, either directly or in an ideological or even glorified form, — to find out these driving forces is the way to get a clue to the laws which govern history as a whole as well as its single periods in the single countries ". To find them out, well and good ; but, as already observed, no one has hitherto succeeded in finding out these hidden forces, and no one has even attempted it. As Engels himself said : " It is not inconsistent to acknowledge that there are ideal forces ; but it is inconsistent not to trace them back to their causes ". Why does he not do so ? It is not enough simply to assure us that the conditions of production or the productive forces are those real causes ; that is not tracing the way back to them, that is skipping it.

Up to this day, all attempts to prove Marx's theory have been equally futile. Environment is of no use : its effects are casual and baffle calculation ; interest, as an intermediate factor, has, in important cases, failed to be decisive. As to institutions, laws and opinions, some of them are determined by conditions of production, while others are independent of them. No last cause has been discovered, no general law has been found. All that has been brought forth to explain history, are abstractions and generalisations of so broad and comprehensive a kind as to become vague and meaningless. Some writers have a partiality for sounding phrases, which give them an illusion of insight. As Goethe said : " Where thoughts are wanting, words are always ready to hand ". Many people are deceived by this method, though not all.

Marx himself having neglected to treat of the decisive question as to how economic conditions are transformed into ideal factors, we had to examine what his followers said on the subject. We applied ourselves in the first place to Engels, who was his collaborator, and to Cunow and Labriola, because these two authors, both university professors, have written systematic works on Marx's historical doctrines. We have seen that everything Cunow has to say on the subject is neither convincing nor does it afford any insight into the problem. He is quite unable to tell us why and how the transformation takes place.

Labriola declares in his turn that " it is not enough to show the real causes, but it must also be demonstrated through what intermediate stages they pass before taking that definite shape in which they manifest themselves as motives in human consciousness, motives whose origin is often blotted out ". He abstains, however, from doing so himself ; it is true that he repeatedly prepares to start, but each time he comes to a standstill in a thicket of vague words, and contents himself with repeating that one should give the necessary proofs. Thus he declares once more, on p. 167, that " the path from the foundations to all the rest, the entire process of mediation and derivation, is very complicated and so tortuous and hidden from our sight as to be not always clearly discernible ". We have heard this before. Finally, on

p. 247, Labriola reveals his secret reason : " he who wishes to trace back the secondary products, like art and religion, to the social conditions, of which they give but an idealised image, would first need to be conversant with that particular social psychology in which the transformation takes place. This will take a long time." There we have it. It seems that to this day nobody has had time enough for this initiation, not even Labriola himself. And his assurance that if only one expended the necessary time one would " at once understand the essence of Egyptian art, of Greek thought, and of the spirit of the Renaissance ", offers no solace for the fact that he either cannot give us the clue or does not want to give it.[1]

The relation between economic conditions and what Marx calls the economic superstructure resembles that between the soil and the plants, growing on a field that we see for the first time. We know that the plants sprang from the soil and that if there was no soil there would be no plants, but we do not know who sowed them, nor where the seeds came from, nor do we know just why these plants grew here and none other. Yet we may say from long experience that many causes beside the soil had to co-operate to make these plants grow.

[1] Marx himself says in the draft mentioned on pp. 3 and 4 that the art of a period does not always correspond to the general development. Yet, he adds, Greek art was based on Greek mythology ; Achilles would be impossible in the age of gunpowder, or Vulcan in that of steam-hammers.

Here, again, it must be said that we did not need Marx to tell us this. All art is expression ; and obviously the artist can give expression only to what has made an impression on his mind and not to things unknown to him. Marx might as well have said that the Greek poets did not write in English, nor the English in Greek. Moreover, it is not the subject that matters in art, but the form given to the subject. And we often find very poor art in times of high social development and wonderful art in primitive times, because the genesis and development of art is determined by quite other elements than economic or social development.

From all these accumulated considerations it is evident that the second, the third and the fourth propositions in Marx's formula must be untenable. We may let the second pass in a restricted sense, admitting that the economic system of a society is the real basis of all legal, political and intellectual phenomena, in so far as these phenomena cannot exist independent of it ; we may even call them a superstructure upon the economic system, just as we may call the plants a superstructure upon the soil, but not in the sense in which Marx and his followers wish it to be understood. As the plants are created *out of* the soil but not *by* the soil, so the ideological superstructure is *erected upon* the economic system but not *created by* it. We may also admit that *some* of the forces of social consciousness correspond to a certain mode of production, but by no means all of them. Only those forms of social consciousness that are directly connected with production, assume a special character which corresponds to it. They constitute, however, only a part of the cultural and intellectual life of a period, and not always the essential and decisive part. Within these limits the second proposition may be accepted. If, however, the words " superstructure " and " forms of consciousness " are understood in the comprehensive sense in which Marx clearly wished them to be accepted, then the proposition is false. It is practically impossible to demonstrate the dependence of all intellectual life on the conditions of production, because no serious scientific investigation of the intricate phenomena and of the countless causal inter-connections in life and history is possible. But whereas it is impossible to prove the theory, it is very easy to refute it, and in numerous cases to prove the non-existence of any such dependence.

The third proposition would have to be altered in so far as " the mode of production of real life " is a condition of social, political and intellectual life ; we shall even admit that it influences the latter to a large extent, but it is false to say that it is its determining cause. Since the same intellectual and other phenomena are compatible with different modes of production and, on the other hand, the greatest differences in intellectual and political life are found, notwithstanding identical mode of production, the latter cannot be the sole determining cause of the former. A causality that is not cogent is no causality at all.

As to the fourth proposition : " It is not man's consciousness that determines his economic and social activity, but it is, on the contrary, his economic system that determines his consciousness ", we have shown that in the general form in which Marx enunciated it, it is false. We shall see later that, in many cases, the reverse is true. Like the productive forces and the conditions of production, man's consciousness and his economic activity influence one another ; there exists a reciprocal inter-dependency between economics and consciousness. That is no new discovery. Bernheim [1] and others have stated this long ago. Marxist authors generally overlook this fact or deny it, contrary to evidence. Sometimes, however, they admit it, though generally without having a clear idea of what this inter-dependency really means. Engels, for instance, says in one of his letters : " All these gentlemen are unschooled in dialectics. They

---

[1] Ernst Bernheim, *Lehrbuch der historischen Methode und der Geschichtsphilosophie* (Leipzig, 1905), ch. vii.

see only cause and effect. They are quite unable to see that this is but an empty abstraction, that polar and metaphysical antitheses of this kind do not exist in the real world except in times of crisis, that the entire great development proceeds by reciprocal action and reaction, that in all this there is nothing absolute, but all is relative. Hegel does not seem to have existed for them. It is of course a reciprocal action of very unequal forces, of which the economic movement is by far the strongest, the most original and the most decisive." [1]

There are several utterances of Engels of a similar purport to be found in his writings, but this one is the most curious. Engels was a man of great-hearted and generous personality, he possessed a thorough knowledge of the circumstances and exigences of the working class and of the political events of his time, he was a keen observer of palpable facts, but, as pointed out before, he was no thinker and his attempts at philosophising are confused and helpless. The passage just quoted is a striking instance. In every sentence he proves himself the dupe of mere words. Setting aside, for the present, the delusiveness of dialectics, which we intend to demonstrate in a separate chapter,[2] we shall only say that, in this passage, Engels seems to misapply the term in the strangest way. What the Marxists call dialectics has nothing whatever to do with the question of cause and effect. To reproach a man concerned with cause and effect in history with being deficient in dialectics is just as reasonable as to take exception to a man investigating the chemical qualities of minerals without being an expert in geology. The long sentence which

---

[1] Letter to Conrad Schmidt of October 27, 1890.
[2] See pp. 200 *sqq.*

follows is pure gibberish. If the relation of cause and effect, considered as such and contrasted with the concrete effect of some real cause, is an abstraction, the dialectic antithesis of two opposed systems or phenomena is certainly no less an abstraction. Why, when Brutus stabs Caesar and Caesar falls, or when the dismissal of Necker and the concentration of troops around Paris causes the Bastille to be stormed by the people, or when a lower tariff causes commodities to grow cheaper, should this be a polar and metaphysical antithesis, and not a very real relation of cause and effect? There is no other way for man to explain history than by the relation of cause and effect, the so-called dialectic method being, as will be shown, a specious self-deception. And how — this part of the sentence is the strangest of all — can the relation of cause and effect or any other "metaphysical antithesis" be true in times of crisis, but not in ordinary times? Are the laws of nature or the laws of thinking different at different times? The entire passage — with the exception of the last sentence, which is merely false — is pure nonsense.

In this last sentence Engels speaks of reciprocal action as something different from the relation of cause and effect. Here again he is deceived, like many another, by a word. The term "reciprocal action" is merely a collective expression for a number of causal actions and reactions between two groups of phenomena. When in some branch of industry — paper, cotton, automobiles, whatever it may be — the necessity of some new substance possessing certain qualities makes itself felt, the effect will be to make scientists study the problem and perhaps discover a substance which possesses the required qualities; this discovery will in turn cause manufacturers to apply new methods, and if it is important, new industries may arise in consequence, larger numbers of workmen find employment, the prosperity of a region or even a whole country may increase, while others, not being able to compete any longer, may suffer and decline. This is the normal action of cause and effect, but arranging in our mind scientific and industrial activities in two groups, we speak of a reciprocal action between them. This, however, is but an abstract general statement, a mere way of speaking, whereas the causal relation between industry and science, and again that between science and the new industrial activities, is a reality and remains exactly the same. To take another example: the experience gained in a war incites inventors to construct more effective firearms, for instance, machine-guns; such a quick-firing gun gives the defensive the advantage over the offensive, whereas before this invention the reverse had been the case; consequently, new tactics are necessary and warfare takes another form. But the new invention and the new tactics can take effect only in the next war, or in the next battle; because time never flows backward and causation only operates in the same direction as time. Grouping, in mind, all arms on one side, in contradistinction to all fighting on the other, we speak of a reciprocal action; yet the reciprocity exists only in our brains; in reality there is only cause and effect.

In the same way, speaking in Chapter II of the mutual inter-dependence of productive forces and conditions of production, and on p. 102 of the same relation existing between economics and consciousness, we meant to say that phenomena belonging to the first of the two groups which are being contrasted with one another, may have a determining influence on phenomena belonging to the second group, and *vice versa*. Men's knowledge and opinions will produce changes in their economic life, and the changed economic life will in turn influence their knowledge and their opinions. The opinions and knowledge, however, which decide that certain persons shall exert a new economic activity, are not identical with the opinions and the knowledge which this economic activity will create in their minds or, perchance, in other minds.

To make this still more clear : supposing group A to consist of the elements a_1, a_2, a_3, a_4, etc., and group B of the elements b_1, b_2, b_3, b_4, etc., a_1 may determine b_1 or b_4, and this may in turn determine a_2 or a_3, but never, if a_1 determines b_1 will b_1 determine a_1, which would be the true reciprocal action. Even when two armies are fighting a battle, there is no true reciprocal action, but every single act has its proper effect, and only because in mind we are considering the two armies as units do we speak of a *reciprocal* action.

What we are wont to call reciprocal action is then but a number of causal actions selected and grouped in a particular way.

The last sentence in that passage of Engels — that " the entire great development proceeds by a reciprocal action of very unequal forces of which the economic movement is the strongest, the primary and the decisive " — is only a repetition of the identical assertion of which no proof is ever given. The sole difference is that, in place of " conditions of production " or " economic basis ", Engels introduces another vague and ambiguous abstraction, the " economic movement ". What is an " economic movement " ? Is the introduction of a new

method in some branch of production an economic movement ? Or was the movement for free trade an economic
movement ? It consisted in a gradual change of men's
opinions, produced by the propaganda of persons who
took a certain view of certain economic problems, and
promoted by distinct economic interests. Or are all
these very different movements and many other economic
phenomena taken together to be considered as " the "
economic movement ? If this be the case — and there
can be little doubt that it was Engels' meaning — then
intellectual and economic elements are so interlocked
and interwoven that it is quite impossible to array and
confront the " ideal phenomena " and the " economic
facts or movements " in two separate categories, as Marx
and Engels do. It is a separation in mind which does
not correspond to anything real ; *it does not exist either
in nature or in history*.

In 1828 Adolphe Blanqui, treating of the situation
of French Agriculture, wrote : " As long as French
peasants know nothing besides the catechism, as long
as their reading is confined to ghost stories and to reports
on miracles, no mulberry tree will be planted in France,
nor will fine wool be produced, nor good horses bred,
nor better agricultural methods introduced ". That is
to say, the mode of production depends on intelligence.
We shall no doubt be able to find economic reasons for
the backward state and the antiquated notions of the
French peasantry in 1828; we shall remember their
oppression and their exploitation by the horrible system
of taxation which was in force in France for centuries.
And we shall also be able to find reasons of an intellectual
and psychological kind for this oppression and exploitation and, above all, for the system of taxation. The

reciprocal action proceeds, ungraspable and inextricably interlaced, through centuries; and, at all times, the mode and conditions of production are at least as dependent on ideology as the reverse.

In Marx's *Capital* there is a passage in which it is said that " the relation of dominion and servitude, though originating directly in the conditions of production, yet in its turn reacts on them and determines them ". It is, of course, false that the relation of dominion and servitude derives its origin from the conditions of production ; [1] yet the flash of truth in this casual remark struck Braunthal, who, reverting to it in his treatise, *Karl Marx as a Philosopher of History*, says : " Then it is not only the mode of production, which determines the political structure of society and so on, but also the reverse. That is certainly something quite new and of great importance for the theory." — " Oh, what a mistake ! " exclaims Cunow — for the works of Marx and Engels are treated by orthodox Marxists as the scriptures and the writings of Aristotle by the scholastics, and it is not reality which is the object of research, but the texts of Marx and Engels which are compared and interpreted — " Braunthal has absolutely misunderstood Marx. There is certainly a reciprocal action, but it proceeds in the following way. The component elements, which derive their origin from the conditions of production, form part of the conditions necessary for the constant renewal of the conditions of production." Translated into intelligible language, this sentence seems to have the following meaning : the conditions of production create an ideological superstructure, that is, conditions of property, of power, of opinions, etc. ; these, in their

[1] Cf. pp. 242 *sqq.*

108

turn, cause a renewal of the conditions of production ; this is how society progresses. If this were true, the mechanism of history would be rather simple : the conditions of production create a certain ideology, this ideology creates new conditions of production, which in turn create a new ideology, and so on. Apart from the fact that all this is pure imagination, that nobody has as yet demonstrated or could ever demonstrate this process, we are afraid that even Cunow would complain of being misunderstood ; he would object that things are not as simple as this, that conditions of production and ideology do not succeed one another in alternating shifts, but exist and work simultaneously, their countless component elements being intertwined and working into each other. To this we would answer in the affirmative and add : yes, it is so, and nobody has to this day been able to extricate this confused entanglement of millions and millions of threads. The solution which Marx and his followers offer in their theory, whether it be rightly interpreted by Cunow or not, is a pale abstraction that has nothing in common with real life. Besides, neither Cunow nor any other orthodox Marxist ever laid much stress on the " reciprocal action " : their attention and all their efforts are devoted to showing that everything comprised in their ideological superstructure is determined by the mode and conditions of production. Engels is the only one to urge a reciprocal action, though with such limitations as to deprive it of all real importance.

It has been our object in this chapter to examine the relations between what is called the economic basis and what is comprised in the term " ideological superstructure ". It may, however, be advisable to note at once that the development of the economic basis itself — the changes in the mode of production — has been left unexplained by Marx. Any Marxist historian would tell us that the different state of civilisation in which Romans and Germans lived, say, at Caesar's time, was due to the difference in the mode and conditions of production prevailing among the two races. If, however, we should ask for the reason why these two kindred races who once had lived under exactly similar conditions of production, nevertheless developed economic and social systems so widely different, if we should ask for the causes determining this divergent evolution, we should receive no answer. It is true that in *German Ideology* Marx — or Engels — derides those who " still cherish the old illusion that it depends only on men's good intentions to change the existing conditions ", adding that " any change in men's consciousness is itself produced by the existing conditions and is a part of them ".[1] This is clearly no explanation, but one of the tautologies in which Marxism abounds. Evidently anything that is new, follows from what already exists. We knew that long ago. What we want to know is, how and why the particular new fact is produced.

We shall see in the next chapter that this gap in Marx's theory is not filled by the fifth or the following propositions.

[1] *Deutsche Ideologie*, pp. 357-8.

CHAPTER IV

THE GREAT SOCIAL REVOLUTIONS

THE essentials of Marx's theory of history are contained in the two first parts (prop. 1-4). In the third part, contained in propositions 5-12, Marx intends to show how the causal connection between the economic basis and the ideological superstructure is apparent in the great social revolutions.

In his fifth and sixth propositions he speaks of contradictions and tensions arising between the productive forces and the conditions of production, owing to the fact that the existing conditions of production block the way to the further development of the productive forces : the consequence is, according to proposition 7, a social revolution, in which, according to proposition 8, following on the changes in the economic basis, the whole enormous legal, cultural and intellectual superstructure is overturned. In propositions 9 and 10, we are told that the ideological forms in which the struggle is fought out, are but illusive, and that we must distinguish between this imaginary and deceptive ideological struggle and the real conflict, which is invariably a struggle between the conditions of production and the productive forces. Propositions 11 and 12 contain further particulars of the nature of these revolutions.

Propositions 5, 6 and 7 are closely connected : " At a certain stage of their development, the material forces of production of a society come into conflict with the existing conditions of production or — what is it but a juristic expression for the same thing — with the system of property within which they have been at work until then. From forms of development of the productive forces, these conditions now turn into fetters of these forces. Then begins a period of social revolution."

Once more, the abstract form which Marx has given to his thought seems objectionable. A conflict between the forces of production, on one hand, and the mode of production or the organisation of production or the system of property on the other, is impossible. There is no conflict possible between electricity or steam power, on one hand, and industry or capital on the other. Conflicts concerning production are possible only between human beings. Men who want to employ steam power may contend or quarrel with others who are against it : workmen whose co-operation is indispensable for the employment of a new force, may enter into a conflict with the employers. Marx, whose doctrine is that historical development is based upon class struggles, was of course aware of this. Accepted in their literal sense, however, the propositions correspond to no real fact in life or history.

What Marx meant was clearly this : the conditions of production and property, as constituted in a certain period by the traditional utilisation of certain productive forces, are disturbed and upset by the introduction of new forces or of a new way of employing the old. The existing conditions of production are apt to prevent or retard the use of the new forces or methods, because the persons, or groups of persons, who profit by the existing mode of production will make a dead set against the introduction of the new forces. The conflict is one between those who wish to preserve existing conditions of production, and those who intend to change them.

Cunow's interpretation is nearly the same. He says : " Such a change does not take place automatically : it arrives within a given form of society with certain traditional institutions and opinions. The new conditions cannot, therefore, develop freely, the old conditions which may still flourish among the greater part of the community, must first be overcome ; and those groups or layers most interested in the preservation of the old conditions of production, will oppose the change." Cunow mentions, as an instance of a similar conflict, the opposition of the ancient guilds and trades to wholesale manufacture. These old guilds of handicraftsmen, he says, had been in their time " useful forms of development of the productive forces ", and he enumerates their various merits, explaining at the same time why and wherefore they were unable to satisfy the demands of modern industry. He describes what pains they took, not only to maintain the ancient guilds, their rules and their obligations, but also how they used every possible means to prevent the expansion of wholesale manufacture and large speculation. He shows how vain all their efforts were ; the capitalists knew how to build up their manufactures and to sell their products in spite of all resistance, until finally it became impossible to maintain the old laws in force and they had to be abrogated.

This concrete instance taken from real history exemplifies the two propositions without proving that they hold good in all cases. It is a well-chosen example of a development in a limited and purely economic sphere. Cunow's description of it is perfectly exact; though when he adds that the people, " as usual ", were conscious only of the ideological elements of the conflict, adducing political, legal and moral reasons for their attitude and for their claims, he falls into error. Both parties were perfectly conscious of the economic nature of the struggle and took their stand chiefly on economic grounds. It was by economic treatises that Dupont de Nemours, Gournay and Turgot waged war against the guilds in the eighteenth century. It was " sous la pression des économistes ", as H. Carré says in his history of the time of Louis XVI, that in the second half of the century the privileges of the guilds were first curtailed and finally abolished. The effect of their writings was not confined to France alone; they also made a great impression in Germany. It is a development that is by no means at an end; the struggle for and against economic limitations, for and against the privileges of corporations, goes on, and each day affords proof of how well aware the parties are of its economic character. That the corporations adduced legal reasons for their privileges, which had a legal character, was perfectly natural. Neither was their citation of political and moral arguments due to an " ideological self-deception "; the introduction of capitalist production had, as the Marxists well know, important political and moral consequences. The relations between buyer and seller and those between employer and workmen underwent a change, which was not always for the better. No doubt the ground was frequently shifted; the adversaries, looking out for allies, joined parties which pursued different aims. All interests, movements and destinies in life are inextricably entangled, and it is scarcely possible for any movement to remain true to purely economic or religious or any other motives. Moreover, in every contest, a good many moral or ideological reasons are set forth which cannot stand the test ; this is human nature ; in a dispute most people are ready to set forth any argument which may have an effect in favour of their particular end. Children do this, proffering the most absurd reasons for not eating food they do not like, or for not going where they hate to go ; and adults do exactly the same. Authors bent on defending an untenable theory, will set forth the most far-fetched arguments and the most sophistical reasons. But this does not prove that men are not aware of the economic nature of their pursuits and struggles, unless that mystical transformation of economic into ideal reasons has previously taken place ; nor does it prove that their ideology is determined by their economic struggles and conditions. Nothing misleads men so much and makes their judgments so unsound as the tendency to generalise an idea founded on a certain experience, without investigating whether it admits of universal application.

It should now be the turn of propositions 6 and 7 ; and we should examine how much truth there is in the assertion that the conditions of production from forms of development of the productive forces turn into fetters of these forces, and whether it is true that times of social revolution will always set in when this happens, and, finally, whether this is the only cause producing such a revolution. This should be our next task. It seems, however, advisable to consider these questions in connection with the historical periods delineated by Marx in propositions 11, 12 and 13. It will be more to the purpose first to investigate whether the process of such a revolution is really as Marx states it to be, in propositions 8, 9 and 10, which run as follows :

" With the change of the economic foundation, the entire immense superstructure is, gradually or rapidly, subverted. In order to understand such a revolution, it is necessary to distinguish between the changes in the conditions of economic production, which are a material fact, open to scientific observation and research, and the legal, political, religious, aesthetic or philosophic, in short, ideological forms in which men become conscious of this conflict and fight it out. Just as we do not judge of an individual by the opinion he has of himself, we cannot judge of a revolution by men's consciousness of it. On the contrary, this consciousness must rather be explained from the conditions of their material life, from the conflict between the social forces of production and the conditions of production."

After all that has been said, the meaning of these propositions appears perfectly clear.

Marx, born in 1818, had grown up under the impression of the French Revolution, the memory of which was still alive and fresh in men's minds ; and he himself witnessed the great economic revolution that followed it. This economic revolution was principally due to the extraordinary progress of natural science, the use of steam power making possible production on a much larger scale than ever before, and affording, at the same time, undreamed of possibilities of transport and communication. It is true that wholesale manufacture had begun as early as the seventeenth century, and that some engines like the mechanical weaving-loom and the spinning-machine had been invented and were in use at the end of the eighteenth century. Yet, the real development of great industry set in only now, and continued with such increasing speed as to change all economic conditions within a short time. The transformation appeared so enormous that the importance of economics was suddenly understood. Economics had always been a practical necessity, and a few thinkers had begun to study the theory; but the public at large had never become clearly conscious of its importance before. Now, men are always inclined to overrate the importance of what happens in their own time and what concerns themselves; and they are also inclined to overrate the importance of new discoveries. Even scientists are apt to believe that some new principle found by them will prove a key to open all locks.

When we consider this general tendency, or rather this mental bad habit, as well as the fact that Marx lived in a period in which occurred the greatest economic and social revolution ever witnessed by man, we shall understand how he came to set himself the task of explaining this revolution, and that he found the explanation in economics and made them the cardinal point of his theory of history.

In reality, this transformation is a ceaseless movement, going on little by little, with imperceptible changes; and only at certain times its pace is accelerated, the movement is sudden and takes violent forms. These sudden accelerations, which we call revolutions, may be due to the most various causes. Besides, it is almost impossible to determine just when a certain movement sets in, what tiny and scarcely perceptible facts or occurrences may be said to form or to betray its beginning, until after a gradual growth through centuries it may cause catastrophes and lead to revolutions. This has been set forth with particular lucidity by Élisée Reclus ; [1] it was, however, no new idea and Marx himself must have known that what we call a revolution is but a period, usually short, of accelerated evolution.

The ruin of the Renaissance in Italy, the Reformation and the religious wars which attended it, and the revolutionary movement in western Europe which lasted from the end of the sixteenth to the middle of the seventeenth century, were all revolutions and catastrophes in no way inferior to the French Revolution. If we form our estimate upon the number of victims and the economic ruin which they caused, they were probably much vaster. But they are long past, faded from the memory of the present generations, waves lost in the sea of time. It is an effect of historical perspective which makes them appear smaller to us.

Now, all these movements, including the French Revolution, are connected and are at bottom only one and the same movement, and none of the later revolutions can be really understood unless those preceding them are also known and understood. Even apart from this consideration, a movement like the French Revolution is itself infinitely complex, consisting of millions of single events, actions and speeches, of countless minor movements and counter-movements of many kinds, yet all intertwined and entangled to such a degree that endless research and an infinite study of details is required to understand its course to some extent. Numerous volumes on various subjects and a good deal of biography

[1] Élisée Reclus, *L'Évolution, la révolution et l'idéal anarchique* (Paris, 1898).

are necessary to give an even approximately adequate idea of it. Moreover, as the effervescence of this wave is still curling the waters, as the consequences of the French Revolution are by no means exhausted or at an end, its features are constantly changing in men's eyes, party interests and individual prejudices influencing their judgment. Supposing an author to proceed by the methods described and stigmatised on page 34, selecting from that sea of events a few particular occurrences forming a special current, leaving out of his consideration all other currents and events, there is scarcely a theory which he might not put forth and pretend to have substantiated by his arrangement of facts.

Cunow, for instance, explains the essence of the French Revolution — and that of the English Revolution also — in the following paragraph,[1] and his appreciation is more or less conformable with the idea which adherents of Marx's theory usually have of it.

" The English Revolution was chiefly a struggle between the wealthy bourgeois class and the gentry turned bourgeois, on one side — the feudal nobility having already been ruined in nearly all parts of England — and Royalty on the other, though the lower classes might at times also be involved in the conflict. In France, however, the critical and revolutionary current, setting in during the second half of the eighteenth century, affected not only the commercial middle class, but gradually imbued almost the entire third estate, including the learned professions, the half-proletarian intellectuals, the handicraftsmen and, in part, even

[1] *Op cit.* vol. i. p. 126.

peasants and workmen, with the same spirit. When the Revolution had broken out in 1789, these pushed aside the liberal Feuillants and the Girondins, the representatives of the commercial middle class of the time, who dwelt in the commercial towns, and they established the Convention, which meant government by the masses. Whereas the English Revolution was, first and foremost, a struggle of the wealthy English citizens to seize power in order to safeguard their particular economic interests, the French Revolution was a struggle of the middle and lower classes of the people against the feudal remnants and fetters of the ' Ancien Régime ' in order to secure better conditions of life."

Obedient to the doctrine that the ideology corresponds to, and is the result of, the conditions of production, Cunow goes on to explain that, owing to the different character of the two revolutions, the political theories of Rousseau and other Frenchmen were imbued with a much more democratic spirit than that of John Locke.

Cunow's appreciation of the two revolutions offers a typical instance of Marxist historiography, which founds the most hazardous speculations upon a very superficial knowledge of a period. Nothing could be more specious and more convenient than these generalisations, which have no foundation whatever in facts. Yet even these generalisations from which all details are eliminated, are full of mistakes, and the real course of events is grossly misrepresented.

The first false statement which strikes us in Cunow's sentences is that on Feudalism in England. A Feudal System similar to that existing on the European continent, especially in France and Germany, never existed in England, and as far as a feudal nobility existed in the country, it was by no means ruined.[1]

The English nobility had been reduced in numbers as well as in power by the Wars of the Roses ; and the influence of the aristocracy was again at a discount during the reign of Queen Elizabeth ; but, favoured by the Stuarts, the nobles quickly regained their ascendancy. Their economic power as well as their political influence remained, except for the few years of Cromwell's Protectorship, unbroken till the nineteenth century. Nay, their position and their influence are, in spite of the progress of democracy, even to-day greater in England than in any other country, Hungary, perhaps, and Japan alone excepted.

Another gross error of Cunow is the idea that the gentry in the seventeenth century had become a part of the middle class. The gentry had no privileges, which

[1] Already under William the Conqueror, all British subjects were bound to swear the oath of fealty to the King directly. Thus the most prominent feature of Continental feudalism, the dependence of each vassal on his immediate lord, in a gradation from the serf up to the sovereign, was, if not entirely abolished, yet deprived of its disintegrating consequences. The English kings invested their vassals with land only, but not with official authority. The political administration of the lands lay in the hands of royal sheriffs ; government was rigidly centralised. The military power of the Kings of England was not based on Feudalism, as on the Continent. In case of war, they did not summon their vassals, but had an army of mercenary soldiers. Their great power enabled them to profit by the return to the monetary system of political economy and to levy high taxes wherewith to pay their armies. The Norman kings of Sicily and the Hohenstaufen as their successors, were the only mediaeval princes on the Continent who were in a position to do the same. Cf. J. H. Round, " The Introduction of Knight Service into England ", in *Feudal England* (London, 1895), pp. 225 *sqq.*, and Hans Delbrück, *Geschichte der Kriegskunst im Rahmen der politischen Geschichte*, vol iii., " Das Mittelalter " (Berlin, 1907), pp. 166-93.

These facts are a further proof that power is not, as Marxism would have us believe, derivable from economics, but rather the reverse ; though the truth is that the relation between both is one of inter-dependency.

the English law accords only to the members of the House of Lords ; but they formed a warlike class of landed proprietors, proud of their descent, the large majority of whom were staunch Royalists and took the king's part.[1]

Moreover, the English Revolution was never and in no way a struggle for power by the wealthy middle classes against Royalty, with the object of furthering economic interests. The English Revolution — unlike the French — was, in its origin, no popular rising ; no class of the people desired a change in the existing order or in the system of government ; it was Royalty attempting a *coup d'état* from above, which the people resisted. The monarchs of western Europe tried, in the course of the sixteenth and seventeenth century, to break the power of the nobles and of the representatives of the people, and to become absolute. Charles I and Lord Strafford wanted to establish in Britain the same absolute power which Richelieu had attained in France for Louis XIII. To carry out his plans the King needed a strong standing army, and to hire and organise such an army he needed money, which Parliament refused. In this struggle for their constitutional rights, the whole nation was unanimous, including a great part of the nobility. When, in course of time, the conflict became more violent, it happened, as it always does in such cases, that the opposition was divided into a more moderate and a more radical wing, a development which was aided and embittered by religious differences. Then the revolution really became — contrary to Cunow's opinion — a war of classes. It was a struggle of the lower classes against

[1] " On the whole, the nobility and gentry took the side of the king ", S. R. Gardiner, *History of the Great Civil War* (London, 1886), vol. i. p. 13.

the King, the nobility, the gentry and the wealthy middle classes who united against them, although, owing to religious and political differences, the two fronts were not always identical with the classes. As ever, some of the leaders of the revolution came from the higher classes : Hampden, Ireton, Pym, Bradshaw, Lambert, and Cromwell himself belonged to the gentry, but the overwhelming majority were of low birth. Cromwell's own brother-in-law, Colonel Jones, had been a servant, Admiral Deane also ; Downing, his Ambassador at the Hague, had been brought up in an orphanage ; General Hewson had been a shoemaker; General Whalley a clothworker; Colonel Pride, who carried out the famous purge of the Long Parliament, a carrier; Colonel Tichborne, a weaver ; General Goffe, a merchant clerk. The most influential members of Cromwell's Council were men of lowest descent ; their enemies never ceased to throw it in their faces. It was a thing that would previously have been quite impossible. It is true that Cromwell himself by no means shared the religious communism of the Levellers ; he had no thought of helping to establish their " Fifth Empire ", he wanted to found a new dynasty and to create a new nobility as Napoleon did later. These, however, were plans and dreams of his ; his real power was based on the loyalty of an army composed of men of the people and led by men of the people. With the economic interests of the wealthy middle classes, the revolution had nothing whatever to do.[1] Nor did the middle classes gain power by it ; the

[1] Not a single merchant was a member of Cromwell's Council of State, and only very few were members of his Parliament. He was not on friendly terms with the City, which disapproved of his policy and of his wars.

It is probable that Cunow or whosoever was his authority, had in mind the Navigation Act, which did indeed further English commerce

political power of the English middle classes dates from the electoral reform in 1832.

Very different was the situation in 1689. The wealthy English middle classes took a serious interest in the " Glorious Revolution ". William of Orange summoned to the Assembly which was to confer the crown of Britain upon him, not only the members of parliament, but representatives of the City also. *He* did so for economic reasons ; he needed money and hoped to get it from them, and they attended the meeting and gave the money for *religious* and *political* reasons.

But even supposing the Revolution to have invested the middle classes with power and brought them economic advantages, it would by no means prove that it had been instigated or fought out for this reason and with this object. That a person is benefited by an action or an event does not prove with any certainty that the event took place or that the action was committed with the purpose of benefiting that person. Railways were neither invented nor constructed for the sake of the land-owners who profited by the compensation paid for expropriated ground. We have noticed already that this kind of vicious reasoning has become a habit with

to an extraordinary degree. But the Navigation Act was passed on October 9, 1651 ; and at the outbreak of the revolution, nine years before, no one had the slightest thought of such a thing. The law had been passed on the instigation of the English Ambassador in Holland, Oliver St. John, and it was meant as reprisals against some offensive acts of the Dutch. The advantages which it brought English commerce, were altogether unexpected and were, moreover, realised only much later. By prohibiting the import of goods on foreign ships, which had been the rule until then and which was now forbidden in order to gall the Dutch, the English were forced to build a great commercial fleet of their own. This, however, was felt as very onerous, and the merchants as a body were very indignant and strongly opposed to the Navigation Act.

Cf. M. P. Ashley, *Financial and Commercial Policy under the Crom-wellian Protectorate* (London, 1934), chs. i. and ii.

Marxists who devote themselves to historical studies. They confuse or identify the consequences of an event with its causes and the effect of an action with its motive, whereas common experience in everyday life as well as the study of history shows that the consequences of men's doings are in most cases very different from what they expected and wished them to be. In those numerous cases, of course, in which our actions are but repetitions of customary acts of which we may have had long experience, the consequences are usually, though not always, to be foreseen. When a man takes the train to Manchester at Euston station, he will probably arrive there, though even in this case something may happen to prevent him from reaching the place, or on his arrival things there may prove very different from what he expected and wished them to be. As soon, however, as a person undertakes something that is not of quite so simple and regular a nature, if he but builds a house, or opens a business, or takes a wife, the results are apt to be widely different from the expectations which were his motive.

We have taken our examples from everyday life, because life and history are chiefly composed of commonplace events and actions, and the closer we investigate the elements composing human life, the surer we shall be of understanding it and of forming opinions which correspond to reality. If, on the contrary, we make sweeping statements without a previous close investigation of what really happened, of the single and simple acts and events which led up to the result, our statements will, in all probability, be false, and the more general they are, the more liable to be erroneous.

For so-called historical actions and events differ from other events and actions of human life chiefly by being recorded. They are either actions of men in conspicuous places, or actions which had such consequences as to seem more than commonly important and to be remembered, but at bottom they are exactly the same as all other acts and events. Our actions become easily "historical" in times of danger, of strife, of uncommon excitement. Then, acts are apt to be remembered and called "historical" which concern the welfare of many people, as, for instance, the attempt at some great change, like the introduction of a new constitution, the installation of a new government, a declaration of war or the conclusion of a peace, and so on. Now, all history is there to prove that the cases are extremely rare in which men really foresaw the consequences of such a change, of a movement or of a struggle; and the reasons, the hopes and intentions which prompted the people to rise, to fight, or to establish a new government, to introduce a new constitution, are nearly always very different from the results of the change. The reason for this is simple: a new institution, a new government, a new law, any new state of things is, according to definition, something of which we have as yet no experience; it is an experience which has to be undergone and of which the results must needs be uncertain. The men, for instance, who, to escape religious persecution or political oppression or from a spirit of adventure left Europe for America, had not the slightest idea that they were laying the foundations of one of the greatest economic and political powers on earth. Neither had the Germans an idea of what they did and what evolution they were preparing when they destroyed the Roman Empire. Historical examples of this kind could be continued to infinity.

Keenly intent, however, upon finding economic causes for every important change in history, the adherents of the Materialist Conception of History adopt a very simple method : the economic consequences of an event, of a movement, of a war, are declared to have been its causes. And they have become nearly incapable of seeing what a monstrous paralogism that is. If, for instance, you point out to them that the English middle classes never thought of furthering their economic interests by the revolution, they will answer : of course they did not think of it ; men do not grow conscious of the real causes ; the English middle classes believed they were fighting for religious and other ideological reasons ; that is the secret of the transformation. And if you reply that they even opposed Cromwell's measures, his wars and the Navigation Act which laid the foundation of their future economic welfare, they rejoin : no matter what they thought or did ; it is so. Or they put it in this way : " It was the historical function of the English Revolution to further the interest and the power of the commercial middle class and to prepare the way for capitalism ". Labriola attributed this function to the Reformation. None of them is conscious of the specious sophistry of the argument.

Of course, when we assume that a higher Power, an Intelligence that is above human comprehension and knowledge, directs events toward certain ends, unknown to us but known to it, and that men are but unconsciously carrying out the will and obeying the directions of this unknown Power, then the Marxist theory is perfectly logical and admissible. For in this case the consequences, pre-existing in that unknown Intelligence which is directing the course of history, are indeed the causes of the events. Adopting this religious and teleological view, we construct a spiritual conjunction between events and their unforeseen consequences, by inserting a conscious and superhuman agency that foresees them. But unless we do this, the whole matter is unthinkable. This assumption, however, or this belief in a conscious spiritual agency is generally rejected by the adherents of the Materialist Conception of History, who assert that all causation in this world is of a " material " nature. Here, however, they are caught in a hopeless contradiction ; for future material causes cannot operate in the present, and intentions or ends are unthinkable unless they exist in some intelligence. There must be somebody to impose the " function " of preparing for capitalism on the Reformation or on the Revolution ; to consider it as self-imposed would mean to attribute intelligence to the movement itself — the terms " movement ", " revolution ", " reformation ", etc., are, however, only collective words designating a million scarcely coherent events, acts, speeches, etc. The ends or consequences of a historical act or movement may exist beforehand as intentions or images in men's brains, or in a higher intelligence ; but intentions or effects which nobody, neither man nor God, thought of or conceived beforehand, and which yet are the causes of these acts and movements, are mere nonsense. Or if you like, this idea of Marxist " thinkers " is a strange kind of involuntary mysticism. As pointed out before, Marx himself did not fall into this error, but expressly rejected it.

What Cunow says about the French Revolution is no less superficial and misleading. It is, in the first place, false that the lower classes " soon after the outbreak of the revolution, pushed aside the liberal Feuillants and the Girondists and established government by the masses ".

It is difficult to say how long the French Revolution lasted. Movements of this kind have no distinct beginning or end. Yet since it is necessary, for practical reasons, to fix these dates in some way or other, we should, I suppose, be justified in assuming that it lasted from the opening of the États Généraux on May 5, 1789, until Bonaparte's first *coup d'état* on October 5, 1795, on which day he crushed the last rising of the common people — that is, six years and five months. Well, it was by no means soon after the outbreak of the Revolution, but more than four years after it, that the Girondists were defeated by Danton, Marat and Robespierre, the leaders of the " Montagne ". The power of the latter lasted only from June 2, 1793 to July 27, 1794, that is, not much more than a year ; but owing to their fearful energy and to the reign of terror which they inaugurated, the domination of these men impressed the imagination of mankind more than any other event of the period. Nevertheless it was only a short and transient episode.

It is further false to mention the Feuillants—moderate Royalists—and the Girondists in the same breath ; neither were the latter representatives of the commercial middle class. The Girondists as well as the Montagnards were Jacobins and fanatical Republicans ; both had voted the measures which inaugurated the " Terreur " ; the dreaded "Comité du Salut Public " had been established by the Girondists. The difference between them and the Montagne rested upon the antagonism between Paris and the provinces ; the Girondists opposed the predominance of the capital. It was, besides, a difference of temper and tactics ; the leaders of the Montagne who, like the Girondists, all belonged to the middle class, thought that in view of the threatening foreign invasion a centralised dictatorship was needed, and they established it, basing their power on the excited masses of the capital. But it was not a difference of class. " The fall of the Girondists on June 2, 1793," says Pariset, " was a *coup d'état* ; that is to say, it was no rising from below, but a struggle on level ground. It did not mean the accession to power of another class or a new generation, but merely that other persons seized the government by violent means. This *coup d'état* of June 2 was a precedent for all later *coups d'état*, up to the 18th Brumaire and the installation of the Empire." [1] To assume that the victory of Robespierre meant the domination of another class, is an arbitrary and distorting interpretation. Marxist historiography is full of similar misinterpretations, mostly due to preconceived ideas and to insufficient knowledge of facts.

There can be no doubt that the French Revolution, contrary to the English Civil War, was a struggle of the middle and lower classes to get rid of the *ancien régime*. It was a true rising from below, a struggle for equal rights and equal fiscal burdens and for the abolition of a governmental and administrative system which had become inefficient and impossible. This way of putting it has the advantage of being conformable with the real facts ; like all such sweeping statements, however, it is inadequate and futile ; it says only what is known to all. The French Revolution was an event of such complexity, its consequences have been so mani-

[1] Cf. E. Lavisse, *Histoire de France Contemporaine*, vol. ii.; G. Pariset, *La Révolution* (Paris, 1930), p. 113.

fold and lasting — they still touch us to the quick — that it is much more difficult to understand and to give an exhaustive definition of it than of the struggle in England a century earlier. Such general phrases give no idea of it.

By saying that my formulation has the advantage of describing the struggle of the French nation in conformity with the facts, I mean that the real demands which the French nation made and for which it fought, are mentioned in it, and not a vague and ambiguous object like Cunow's " better conditions of life ".

It appears necessary in this connection to expose another grave error in the propositions of Marx.

It is entirely false that " the changes in the conditions of economic production can be observed and determined with the precision of natural science ", — contrary to " the legal, political, religious, artistic or philosophic, in short ideological, forms in which men become conscious of the conflict and fight it out ". Rather the opposite is true. It is the legal and political conflict that can be observed and determined with the precision almost of natural science. The old forms exist palpably and visibly, as laws and institutions ; the changes aimed at are evident from demands, petitions, speeches, pamphlets, etc. ; the actual results of the conflict are again to be stated in the form of new laws and new institutions. Even the purely ideological, the philosophical and religious conflicts are well known to us, every shade of philosophical and religious opinion, every dissension, being expressed and registered for posterity in countless books, treatises and speeches. All the changing and conflicting thoughts and views are clearly discernible.

Very different is the case when we proceed to economic

conditions. It is true that in our time, in which a great many persons devote themselves to the study of economic conditions and statistic material is superabundant, it is in most cases possible to be more or less exactly informed, though even to-day the causes as well as the consequences of changes that occur are not always easy to discover and are frequently open to controversy, while the changes themselves are often so gradual that for a long time they escape our notice. Yet, on the whole, we are now well aware of economic conditions and we are perfectly conscious of the characteristics of our system of economics. Of the past, however, we know but little ; history, so far as economics is concerned, is mute. Up to the first half of the nineteenth century, statistics were neglected and in their infancy ; our knowledge of the economic conditions of former times is desultory and in every way inferior to that of all other spheres of life in the past. We have constantly to fall back upon inferences and conjectures. Concerning all that Marx calls the superstructure, we are fairly well informed ; there are plenty of documents and the sources are inexhaustible ; whereas our notions of what, according to him, is alone important, the economic foundations, are comparatively small and inconsiderable.[1]

[1] After immense toil and industry during long years of patient research, G. d'Avenel has, in his *Histoire économique de la propriété, des salaires, etc. en France* (vols. i.-v., Paris, 1892 *sqq.*), collected the most important economic data for the period from 1200 to 1800 in France. Other students have attempted similar, though not equally comprehensive, works concerning other times and countries. It seemed impossible to Avenel to find reliable and exact data in sufficient quantities for dates prior to 1200.

A small quantity of data and facts are extant from antique times concerning some of the regions which belonged to the Roman Empire. From a thousand years of Roman history scarcely half a dozen economic treatises have reached us. As to the vast regions outside the Roman Empire, we have to content ourselves with a few statements and with inferences from

In spite of this ignorance economic conditions might nevertheless be the decisive factor in history. But the assumption that they can be stated with more precision than all other historical phenomena is utterly false. The case, at least for the past, is just the reverse.

This assertion is followed, in the same proposition (10), by a simile intended to illustrate and support it, though it is no less incongruous than the assertion itself. Marx says : " As little as an individual can be judged by the opinion he has of himself, just so little can a revolution be judged by men's consciousness of it ".

We do not know what another individual really is, as little as he knows it himself ; our judgment is liable to be as mistaken as his own. Moreover, the opinion a man has of himself is rarely known to us, and we depend for our judgment of him on the impression he makes on us by his utterances and actions. Now, this corresponds exactly to what Marx, speaking of society, calls the ideological superstructure. Marx's simile turns against him.

As far as we are able to ascertain the consciousness and the opinion which the men who made — and lived through — the French Revolution had of the conflict, we discover an ideology which is indeed far from corresponding to reality. The revolutionaries were convinced that they had found eternal truths and were fighting for the salvation of mankind ; they imagined they were making ready a paradise on earth, just as Marx and Engels expected it from socialistic reforms. These are indeed ideologies. The adverse party, who

records of another nature. Considering the scarcity of records, these inferences which fill many volumes of economic history, are an admirable proof of the perspicacity of men's intellect and of scholarly application.

opposed the revolution, believed in their turn that they were fighting for established rights, for justice, order and morality; in short, they likewise imagined that the salvation of society depended on their victory. This was, of course, only another ideological self-deception. If Marx had this in mind, we should agree with him perfectly, but unfortunately the above-mentioned ideologies form but the smallest part of what he calls the ideological superstructure.

Before we proceed with our inquiry into the French Revolution, we shall further illustrate the subject by giving another striking instance of the same phenomenon. When the mediaeval Emperors believed themselves to be the successors of the ancient Roman Emperors, and all the world shared their opinion, this was indeed mere " consciousness " and an " opinion they had of themselves ". Yet their eternal conflicts with the Popes, their expeditions to Rome, though caused by a false and illusive ideology, were very real historical events, which can be " observed and determined with the precision of natural science ". And these events, as well as the ideology which had produced them, had momentous consequences for Germany and Italy and for all Europe.

Let us now revert to the French Revolution. It seems doubly important to understand the French Revolution, because its influence on mankind in the nineteenth century can hardly be over-estimated, and because the revolution and the events which followed it, led Marx to the conclusions on which he based his theory.

We can but repeat that it is impossible really to understand the French Revolution unless its connection with events that happened several hundred years before it, is plainly understood. We must retrace the history of France and its institutions to the very beginnings. Royalty in Britain was very powerful after the Norman Conquest, so powerful that the nobility and the commons united against it and soon forced it to grant a constitution which Royalty never succeeded in abolishing, because lords and commons were always united whenever the rights which they had obtained at the point of the sword, were in serious danger. In France, however, the reverse had been the case. Royalty had been very weak at the beginning ; and in order to maintain their rule against the too-powerful nobles, and to extend it, the kings sought the support of the middle classes. In no country, perhaps, were the rights and the power of the bourgeoisie in the Middle Ages greater than in France. In the sixteenth century the administration as well as the right of judicature was almost wholly in the hands of the bourgeoisie ; the nobles, though still powerful, had to be content with military posts and offices at court. The Duke of Saint-Simon, particularly indignant at this state of things, called the reign of Louis XIV in the seventeenth century, "un long règne de vile bourgeoisie". This development had suffered a short interruption in the first half of the seventeenth century. French Royalty made an attempt to render its power absolute and, as in England, nobility and middle class united against it. Yet this union, which in England was maintained through five hundred years, was in France only of brief duration. Before two years had passed the rupture between nobles and bourgeois was complete. Another circumstance, however, was decisive. Genius in France fought for Royalty, which found eminent champions in Richelieu and Mazarin, whereas in England genius was only to be found in the revolutionary ranks from which Cromwell emerged to become their head. Victorious Royalty became all-powerful in France. Louis XIV has always been regarded as the prototype of an absolute monarch. Yet he continued to govern the country by means of the bureaucracy; the nobles had to be obsequious courtiers or military officers as before. The civil officers, however, though of bourgeois descent, had, from human vanity, which plays no slight part in history, always striven after ennoblement; and, as many an office conferred nobility on the person holding it, a part of them had been merged in the old *noblesse*, while another portion formed a special class as the *noblesse de robe*. In the meanwhile, however, a new middle class had arisen, merchants, lawyers and writers, who stood waiting on the threshold, feeling themselves excluded from society and its privileges and enjoyments. For a long space of time they had not resented this; deference to nobility had been so complete and the distance that separated the classes, so immeasurable that it seemed impossible to bridge it over. Only some very rich bankers and a few successful writers could cross it; the rest had been content to make money and were too modest to ask for more. Since then, however, printing and the sale of books had very much increased. Many men of the new middle class were now educated, and knowledge and culture gave them a higher opinion of themselves. Feeling themselves the equals and even superiors of the nobles, they began to regard the honorary privileges of the latter as an insult, while their real privileges, consisting in an exclusive right to commissions as higher officers, and to the higher positions in the civil service, meant serious disadvantage to the young men of the middle class, precluding them from a great career, and were felt as another insult. This was felt all the more as just at this time, probably because the ruling classes were afraid of the qualities and pretences of the middle class, the exclusion became complete and was established as a law. Under Louis XIV there had been exceptions ; archbishops, ministers and marshals of low birth, like Bossuet, Séguier, Le Tellier, Colbert, Catinat and others had been appointed. During the second half of the eighteenth century, however, not a single bishop had been ordained who was not of noble birth. All the higher judges were nobles ; and in 1781 a decree of Maréchal de Ségur, minister of war, provided that only a nobleman could become a lieutenant in the army. One may imagine the rage which this decree roused in the middle class.[1] As a fact, ruling classes nearly always show a narrow-minded tendency to close their ranks and shut the door upon all outsiders, oblivious of the fact that their retention of power depends on the reception and absorption of all the talent available in the community.

Even this might not perhaps have proved insupportable if the ruling bodies had proved efficient. But absolute government, as is invariably the case, had stifled all initiative or rendered it hopeless. Reforms became less and less possible because there was nobody to carry them into effect. Beset with privileges and traditions, it was an absolutism that obstructed its own power. The bureaucracy, consisting of officials whose posts were hereditary, formed an exclusive caste, jealously watching their privileges and imbued with the haughtiest *esprit*

[1] Cf. Louis Madelin, *Le Crépuscule de la monarchie* (Paris, 1936), pp. 217-19.

de corps. Conservative, as officials naturally are, they opposed and resisted all reforms in the administration of justice as in civil administration. It was a fatality that just in the period of absolute power the most incapable monarchs were called to govern France. Capable and incorruptible men were either not appointed or did not remain in office; favouritism prevailed; the conduct of public affairs was in the hands of royal mistresses or court coteries. The mismanagement grew constantly worse, making its effects felt, and discontent became general.

A great part of the French nobility was ruined and hopelessly in debt. Part of the middle class had enriched themselves by commerce. Indigence prevailed in many provinces among the peasants. " In France there is general want," wrote the Marquis de Mirabeau several years before the revolution, estimating the number of those who lived by begging at no less than 20 per cent of the population; the lowest estimate is over 10 per cent; that would mean between three and five million unemployed in a population of not quite twenty-six million. The French State itself was bankrupt and had been so for a long time, the deficit becoming heavier every year. The system of taxation had at all times been the worst imaginable. The nobility, the clergy, officials and many others were exempted from paying taxes. Two hundred thousand privileged persons, owning two-thirds of all the property in France, paid no taxes. The entire amount of these weighed upon the poorer classes, particularly the peasants. The method of collecting the taxes was absurd, expensive for the state and ruinous to the tax-payers. The revenue was quite insufficient for a State maintaining a great standing army, a large number of officials, and the most expensive of Courts. In the seventeenth century, the Marshal of Fabert, and after him, the Marshal of Vauban had in vain elaborated masterly schemes for the introduction of a general land- and income-tax ; the system made it impossible to carry such ideas into effect.

For the State had already been bankrupt in the seventeenth century, and the deficit had been enormous even then. The greater part of the nobility at the time of Louis XIV was poor ; and if a small section of the middle class knew how to enrich themselves, the people in the mass were miserably poor. The number of those who lived on alms was extreme. " All France ", wrote Fénélon, " is one big almshouse and hospital." In the year 1765, Bossuet, in his capacity as archbishop of Paris, wrote a confidential letter to Louis XIV, in which he said : " If there is no remedy for this evil, all is lost beyond hope of recovery ". The peasants revolted from sheer hunger, there were ceaseless small risings in the provinces, risings in which the dead sometimes numbered several thousands. In fact, conditions in France had been much worse in the seventeenth century than towards the end of the eighteenth, on the eve of the revolution. The inward mental structure, however, had not yet been shaken ; the era of criticism had not begun ; the tradition of obedience, the belief in authority, was still powerful in the souls of men.

In the eighteenth century the French people were better off ; wealth was growing in general until 1786, in which year the commercial treaty with England, concluded between the French Government and Sir William Eden, resulted in the import of cheap English commodities and caused an economic crisis. A great number of manufacturers and business men went bankrupt and unemployment rose to a dangerous height. To make matters worse, a series of bad harvests followed. This, however, though it certainly made the people more restless, was not decisive. As Cunow rightly says, a critical and revolutionary current had set in about the middle of the century. Whereas, in the seventeenth century, a current of influence emanated from the Court of Versailles, a current in the minds of men which made them admire and imitate the splendour and power of Louis XIV, so that absolutism became general on the continent, in the eighteenth century a mental current emanated from England and made men admire and wish to imitate liberal institutions. Habits of thought are very contagious. In the seventeenth century it had been absolutism ; nowadays it is communism or fascism ; in the eighteenth century it was liberalism. And it was the French nobility which, much more than the middle classes, became imbued with liberal opinions, a fact which seems to have escaped Cunow. The readers and admirers of Voltaire and Rousseau were to be found, above all, in the aristocracy. Madame d'Épinay, the Duke and Duchess of Montmorency-Luxembourg and the Marquis of Girardin were the successive protectors of Jean-Jacques Rousseau ; offering him hospitality in their country houses and making it possible for him to exist and to write his books. There was, in addition to this, the prodigious effect of the American War of Independence. Many French noblemen took service in the rebel army and later on carried home and propagated the political convictions for which they had fought in the other hemisphere. The nobility were the first to demand constitutional government in France.[1] Vilfredo Pareto is of opinion that the downfall of the *ancien régime* was caused by the ruling classes having adopted opinions contrary to their interests and to their power, by which their force of resistance was paralysed.[2] While Cunow forgets to mention the nobles among those imbued with the new spirit, he is committing another gross error in saying that the revolutionary current had affected " not only the commercial middle class but almost the entire third estate ". This sentence contains a double fallacy. For the commercial middle class was the least revolutionary part of the whole nation. They had not the slightest reason for discontent, being furthered and favoured by the government in every possible way.[3] They were endowed with privileges, received subventions and honours ; the highest nobility, the royal princes themselves took part in founding new industries ; far from fettering industry and the productive forces,

---

[1] A very important part in preparing the political revolution was played by the Freemasons. Almost all educated persons, a great part of the aristocracy, and even a good many Catholic priests belonged to them. Cf. Louis Amiable, *Une Loge maçonnique d'avant 1789* (Paris, 1897); Louis Madelin, *Le Crépuscule de la monarchie* (Paris, 1936) ; and the brilliant biography of Paul Jones by Valentine Thomson, *Le Corsaire chez l'Impératrice* (Paris, 1936).

[2] Cf. Pareto, *Traité de Sociologie générale* (Paris-Lausanne, 1917), p. 1406. The fact is certainly true, though it is but a part of the truth. Pareto is, moreover, mistaken in his belief that the Royal Government and the Royalist nobility did not dare or wish to make a stand and employ force against the revolution. They tried it repeatedly, but generally at the wrong moment and, owing to the irresolution of the king, half-heartedly, and were also handicapped by the growing indiscipline of the troops. In the Vendée, however, their resistance cost France several hundred thousand dead and endangered the existence of the Republican government.

[3] " French industry existed only owing to initiative and furtherance on the part of Royalty ", P. Mantoux, *La Révolution industrielle*, p. 5. Cf. Carré, " Histoire de Louis XVI. Le Régime Économique ", in Lavisse, *Histoire de France*, vol. ix. pp. 203 *sqq.*

the government did all that was in its power to encourage them.[1]

[1] The Revolution gave origin, in its turn, to a new commercial class which took its side and had every interest in doing so, since it had grown rich by buying the confiscated estates of the noblemen and the Church. This class, however, did not exist before the revolution.

We ought to mention the perfectly erroneous and misleading articles of Kautsky's, " Die Klassengegensätze von 1789 ", in the *Neue Zeit*, 1889, pp. 1, 49, 97, 145.

Kautsky admits that conditions at the time of the Revolution were infinitely complex and even contradictory, that all classes and sections of the French nation were divided among themselves, that there were no clearly defined battle-fronts, that many acted against the interests of their own class, and that opinions did not always harmonise with class interest.

Having thus stated the truth, he proceeds nevertheless to explain the entire movement from the point of view of class interests. Closely examining his somewhat confused description of events, we arrive at the following bewildering result :

The great financiers, the owners of monopolies and industrial establishments, the manufacturers, the traders and, finally, the guilds (that is, the entire commercial class), were in favour of the *ancien régime*, they adored the system founded on privilege—yet Kautsky is of opinion that the Revolution was made with the object of effectuating the demands of this class. The mass of the people who made the Revolution, could not cease to fight for it, because if they had done so, the commercial class would have been victorious (!). Therefore they established a reign of terror, which could not possibly be of long duration. On the whole, the Jacobins were doomed to failure because their rule and their politics blocked the way to capitalist revolution. The final result is that the capitalists who had been against the Revolution, owed their victory to this very Revolution which, though their interests were bound up with the *ancien régime*, was made in their interest. Of course, Kautsky did not say this in so many words—otherwise he would have become aware of its inconsistency, but divers passages of his articles contain these judgments. It is, at bottom, the same sophistry which we have noted before, the consequences of the entire movement being taken for its causes.

For, as pointed out above, a capitalist class that owed its existence to the Revolution was the consequence. The persons who had grown rich by buying and selling the confiscated property, were able to make enormous profits from the armaments and issues required for the Napoleonic wars, and the great public works commenced in this period, as well as by speculating, for which the Continental System afforded ample opportunities. The enrichment of the middle classes after the Revolution made the Marxists believe and claim that the Revolution itself was made by the pre-revolutionary

Neither were the French workmen affected by the critical current, though their condition had gone on deteriorating since the sixteenth century. How should they be ? They did not read books and pamphlets like the upper classes; meetings with lectures and speeches were unknown to them. They were not revolutionary-minded until 1786 ; the crisis and unemployment made them discontented. Neither did the peasants think of revolution. They desired to become owners of the soil, and to be freed from immoderate taxation, from the tithe and the *corvées*, but they did not think of bringing this about by violent means and they revolted only when they were miserable and starving. It was the educated people, to whichever class they might belong, who were really revolutionary-minded. In all classes, however, there was a certain restlessness ; the psychic foundations of the great majority of Frenchmen were crumbling ; the suggestion of authority was no longer the same ; they no longer believed that all was right in the world.[1] The entire nation was like an army which has lost confidence in its officers, or like an edifice the connection of the single stones of which is loosened ; any shock made with a certain force may cause its fall. And yet commercial middle class, which never had the slightest intention of making it and was by its very interests bound to be dead against it.

One might as well say that the discovery of America by Columbus was due to the capitalist class because there are at present many millionaires in the United States.

[1] How great the change was, may be inferred by recalling La Bruyère's words, written in the seventeenth century, " The people has so blind a prejudice in favour of the great lords, people are so generally enraptured by their appearance, their movements, the tone of their voice, that if they only had a mind to be good, they would be deified ", and comparing with it what people a century later thought and said of the nobles and their privileges. La Bruyère himself had criticised the great from a moral, never from a political, point of view. Cf. La Bruyère, *Les Caractères*, vol. ii., " Des Grands ".

Danton's words, " La République était dans les esprits vingt ans avant sa proclamation ", was true only of some intellectuals. The whole nation, from the nobility down to the peasants and the workmen, loved the king, and no one dreamt of overthrowing the monarchical system. What the people demanded was a complete reform of the government and of the administration. The belief in existing institutions, in the entire social structure with its gradation from the throne down to peasant and workman, was shaken ; only the throne itself seemed safe and trustworthy. It was from the king that reform, a marvellous reconstruction of France, was expected. That this last confidence was lost in the course of events, was due to fatal mistakes which the royal family and its advisers committed during the first two years of the revolution. " Never was a king of France so beloved by his people ", says Lavisse, "as Louis XVI was after summoning the States General." [1]

Economic reasons and the system of taxation in particular, played an important part in causing discontent ; for, when the great majority of the people are well off, the masses are, as a rule, disinclined to revolutionary actions. It is also perfectly true that production in general was shackled and impeded by unreasonable laws and by a corrupt and rotten system of administration. This, however, had been the case in France and in many other countries for centuries without causing a revolution. In the eighteenth century itself the system was nearly or quite as bad in most countries of Europe, yet in none of them did a revolution break out. Those " real causes " of Marx are of a curious kind, effective

[1] Cf. E. Lavisse, *Histoire de France*, vol. ix. 1, " Le Règne de Louis XVI " (Paris, 1910), p. 431. Cf. also Louis Madelin, *op cit*. pp. 206 *sqq*.

in one country and perfectly ineffective in others.[1] On the other hand, we are unable to find that there had appeared any new productive forces in France, or that a change in the conditions of production should have created a new ideology. There had been no substantial change in the productive forces during the last centuries ; a great industry scarcely existed, and the government, far from putting any obstacles in the way of the few big establishments and wholesale manufacturers that existed, did its utmost to smooth the ground for them. Neither had the conditions of production undergone any substantial change ; the distribution of economic power and influence was more or less the same as it had been a hundred years before. It was the changed ideology that brought about the revolution and, through the revolution, produced new laws and new conditions of property and, finally, as a further consequence, a complete change in the conditions of production. The peasants had conquered the soil and from mere tenants had become owners of the land ; the middle class had obtained political and economic liberty. When, *after* the political and legal changes, owing to the discoveries of scientists, steam and electricity were made subservient to man and put to use, there did indeed follow a vast economic change. And now the middle class became rich and powerful and partly predominant.[2]

[1] " Absolute Monarchy was in the seventeenth century an economic necessity ", says Mehring, *op cit.* p. 442. He does not say why, nor does he explain why it was no economic necessity in England or in Sweden.

[2] The predominance of the middle classes in the nineteenth century was only partial, because, owing to purely ideological factors, to tradition and to the habitual deference to nobility in the minds of the large majority of the people, the feudal aristocracy retained a large part of its influence.

It is impossible, as observed before, to understand events unless the

It was by no means the productive forces that had broken their fetters ; the productive forces had remained

political and economic development in France from the beginnings is understood and kept in mind.

Until the thirteenth century almost all persons in France who were not noble, were serfs, the inhabitants of the towns, which at this time were small and poor, alone excepted. Even many noblemen were serfs. The serfs were not badly off ; as they represented the wealth and the power of their lords they were generally well treated.

At the end of the thirteenth century the enfranchisement of the peasants began, and it went on without interruption for three centuries. At the end of the sixteenth century the great majority of the French peasants were free tenants and only a small number remained serfs.

Though favoured by moral and religious views, the enfranchisement was essentially due to economic reasons. There was plenty of untilled soil, but only few field hands ; in order to induce the peasants to clear the land and cultivate it, the owner had to offer them the property of the tilled land on condition that they should pay him certain not very considerable dues, mostly in kind, sometimes in money. The consequence was a legal state of double property. The land which belonged for ever to the free peasants who had reclaimed it from the wilderness, remained nevertheless the property of the lord to whom the dues were paid.

Now, while the dues, whether consisting of money or of a certain quantity of fruits or a number of fowls, remained invariably the same as once imposed in the original agreement, the value of the soil was constantly increasing. This economic process went on uninterruptedly for six hundred years, from the thirteenth century up to the Revolution. It was a development that was clearly unfavourable to the landed proprietors and advantageous for the peasants. It was one of the reasons contributing to the ruin of the French nobility.

In the sixteenth century, however, the nobles acquired a new privilege, namely, the exclusive right of hunting which hitherto had been free to everyone. This right, which for the nobles was a question of prestige, affording them an amusement, but no economic advantage worth mentioning, was a heavy burden on the peasants, whose fields were ravaged by the game as well as by the hunters. The dues and the compulsory labour—the so-called *corvées* — had become unimportant and of small amount, yet, owing to the changed ideology, they were now regarded as unjust and oppressive, whereas at the time of their institution they had seemed small in comparison with the gift of the land and of personal freedom.

Yet this was not what the peasants most resented ; the rights of the lords of the manor, though they might be odious, were relatively slight and could be borne with ; the really unbearable economic burden that ruined the peasants was taxation. In feudal times the lord of the manor had been the government ; the dues which were paid to him replaced the passive as ever ; but a new ideology in men's brains had broken the fetters and had made possible the use of new productive forces and the formation of new conditions of production. The best proof of this is that in 1810, more than twenty years after the revolution, there were in use in France but two hundred steam engines,

taxes paid to the government. He protected the tenants in case of an attack by an enemy, he administered justice, his was the police ; as for cultural achievements, like the building and upkeep of public roads or schools, nobody thought of asking for it. But no peasant paid taxes to the king.

In the course of time, however, things had changed. Of the feudal system there remained a mere façade, behind which the reality had crumbled. Feudalism had been first and foremost a military organisation and a system of government. Now the state had taken over the government as well as the military concerns, and raised very high taxes in order to be able to maintain a standing army. The nobility and the clergy being exempt, these taxes had to be paid by the middle class and by the peasants. The peasants, however, who in former days had been well aware of the reasons why they paid dues to their lords, were now utterly unable to understand why they should pay such exorbitant taxes to the state.

As for the workmen, wages had constantly fallen since the sixteenth century, whereas the prices of bread and of most commodities had as continuously risen. From the time of Henry IV up to Napoleon, though the costs of the most necessary means of subsistence were but 40 per cent of what they were at the end of the nineteenth century, the actual value of wages was not even the third part of what it was later. The French workman in town as well as in the country was badly housed, badly dressed and badly fed ; he was scarcely in a position to eat meat three times a year.

The reason for this unlucky change was, in the first place, the extraordinary growth of French population, with which the production of goods had been unable to keep pace ; and secondly, the devaluation of money after the discovery of America. Yet nobody was aware of these causes. What everybody saw and felt was the misery of the people, the privileges and the mismanagement of the higher classes. Both, privileges and mismanagement roused the middle and lower classes to fury, and they rose against them. These were the causes of the French Revolution.

The German peasants in the eighteenth century were, in every respect, more miserable than the French ; they were still serfs, whereas the French peasants were free landowners ; yet they made no revolution.

Cf. G. d'Avenel, *op. cit.* vol. i. Book II, " La Terre ", and vol. iii. Book III, " Les Salaires " ; and Georg Ludwig von Maurer, *Geschichte der Fronhöfe, der Bauernhöfe und der Hofverfassung in Deutschland* (Erlangen, 1862-3), vol. iv. pp. 521 *sqq.*

while in Prussia there were but two in all as late as 1822. The first practicable steamship sailed on the Hudson in the year 1807 ; about the same time the first locomotive made its appearance. In England, matters were different. The English Revolution having been fought out in the seventeenth century, there was a high degree of political liberty in the land, and, consequently, of economic liberty also. Thus, the steam engine had long ago been put to use, and their number in 1800 was estimated at no less than 5000.[1]

The succession of events is now clear : first came, about the middle of the eighteenth century, a purely ideological revolution in France ; half a century later there followed the political revolution, enforcing a complete change of the legal order. Not before all these changes had been accomplished, did the great economic change set in. This time, to be sure, it may be examined and studied with scientific precision, because economic science had made enormous progress at the same time. The evolution and the succession of events is exactly the reverse of what Marx and the Marxists claim it to be.

The economic revolution which succeeded the political upheaval had ideological consequences in its turn and produced a good number of varied illusions and self-deceptions. One of the most noteworthy ideological phenomena derivable from it is the Marxist theory of history.

We may, at any rate, rest assured that the " contradictions of material life " and the conflict between productive forces and conditions of production con-

---

[1] " The modern factory system began in England in the last third of the eighteenth century ", Mantoux, *op. cit.* p. 1.

tributed only in a slight degree to the causes of the French Revolution, while in the English Revolution in the seventeenth century they played no part whatever.

It has been pointed out before that to speak of a conflict between forces and conditions of production is merely metaphorical and that a conflict of this kind does not take place in reality. In real life conflicts are possible only between persons who are desirous of using either the known or newly found productive forces in another manner than the existing conditions of production and of property permit, and therefore feel prompted to change these conditions — and those persons who desire to preserve them unchanged. We did not fail to add that Marx was aware of this and that it may even have been his real meaning ; but the abstract form in which, owing to the fatal influence of contemporary German philosophy, he chose to express himself, proved dangerously misleading to himself as well as to his followers. Instead of examining the concrete facts of life and history, they went on discussing events in the abstract, taking their abstractions for realities, and so arriving necessarily at results as unreal and imaginary as those of the scholastics. We have seen that Marx declares, in the 9th proposition, that men become conscious of economic conflicts in ideological forms and fight them out in these forms. We quoted Mr. John Strachey, giving an instance from the French Revolution, telling us that " it is only if we go behind this ideology that we discover that it has grown up out of the conflict between changing, developing, technical and economic conditions and a static political structure. It is only then that we shall recognise that what the victory of the idealists will do, is to bring the political structure into line with the technical and economic developments which have taken place." We have shown that it is nothing of the sort, that the technical and economic developments followed after the political structure had been brought into line with ideology. We may add that, as far as the struggle is of an economic nature, men are plainly conscious of it, though it is true that they frequently deceive themselves as to their importance and their consequences. It is equally true that economic conflicts are apt to spread to other spheres and sometimes to shift ground entirely, just as, in other cases, conflicts of a very different nature may affect economic interests and end by turning wholly or partially into economic conflicts. It is further clear that economic interests and reasons are apt to be draped with moral or religious pretences, though it may also and frequently happen that moral and religious considerations coincide with economic interests. When starved workmen demand higher wages, moral and religious reasons may be in favour of their economic interests. As a rule, however, it may be said that men are conscious of economic conflicts in their true nature and without any disguise. The countless risings, armed conflicts, and wars which, since remotest ages, were consciously fought for purely economic reasons, for booty, for the ownership of the soil, for the remission of debts, taxes, tributes, etc., for and against customs duties, struggles for higher wages and against exploitation, for and against economic privileges and monopolies, for and against the prohibition of whole industries in certain countries or provinces — as, for instance, that of wool-spinning and cloth manufacture in Ireland — must make this clear to anybody who does not purposely shut his eyes to facts. There is, indeed, nothing of which men are in general more quickly aware than of economic advantages or losses ; no ideological form is needed to make them conscious of these. Anybody who, instead of making abstract statements, studies the real history of the French Revolution, will find that the economic demands of the people were put forward plainly, directly and consciously. They demanded equal and just taxation, higher wages and shorter working-hours, the abolition of all economic privileges, the confiscation of the patrimony, liberty of work and commerce, the abrogation of all inland duties and of all protective duties ; thus distinctly claiming the liberation of the productive forces, or rather of production, from all obstructive fetters. As far as this was their object and as far as it was accomplished, it was no hidden process, disguised in ideological slogans : it was openly proclaimed and openly put into effect. All these economic problems played a large part in the debates of the Constituent and the Legislative Assembly as well as in those of the Convention, and the reports in the *Moniteur* are full of them.

But as to the other objects for which men fought in the Revolution, liberty of thought and conscience and free institutions being but economic objects in disguise, or caused in some mysterious way by the development of the productive forces and consequent economic difficulties, this is a perfectly gratuitous assertion.

What frequently happens is that the consequences of an economic act or law appear only at a time when their causes have sunk into oblivion, just as actions or habits of an adult person might often be explained from forgotten events that took place in his childhood. One of the most tragic and fatal events in European history was the gradual ruin and expulsion of the peasantry from the estates of the feudal lords and other great landowners in almost all countries of Europe, a movement which in some countries began earlier and in others later. In England it began in the sixteenth century. It was originally a purely economic measure; the great landowners in Spain, England and elsewhere found sheep-breeding more lucrative than agriculture, and for this reason they expelled their tenants and depopulated the country. The poor people, being beggared, migrated into the towns : this was the origin of the modern proletariat. As many of them, finding no employment, became tramps, the most pitiless and cruel laws were made against them. They were condemned to be whipped, sometimes to be hanged, or were made the serfs of any master who claimed them. The persons who framed these laws had certainly long forgotten the circumstances which had been the origin of this nuisance ; they probably believed they were supporting public morality by punishing people who were " loath to work " and infested the country. The cruelty of the penalties was in accordance with the spirit of the period. Nobody has given a more heartrending description of these events than Marx himself.[1] The men who made these cruel and stupid laws, were themselves unaware of the economic character of this disastrous phenomenon ; they had no idea where this invasion of tramps came from ; but then, this was decades later, whereas at the time of the expulsion of the peasant families, the landowners knew

[1] Cf. Marx, *Capital*, vol. i. ch. xxiv., " Primary Accumulation " ; and W. J. Ashley, *An Introduction to English Economic History and Theory* (2nd ed. London, 1893), vol. ii. ch. iv., " The Agrarian Revolution ".

perfectly well that they were acting from economic reasons.[1]

The counterpart to the expulsion of the peasants was that of the Moors from Spain in the sixteenth century and that of the Huguenots from France in the seventeenth, for, whereas the former was enacted for economic reasons and brought those who expelled the tenants large profit, the latter two events had purely ideological causes and had grave economic consequences for those who perpetrated them.

All economic changes and conflicts, however, invariably call forth changes in the distribution of power and *vice versa*. And the distribution of power having the greatest influence on the distribution of wealth, economic conflicts are apt to become political and the reverse. No one will ever understand history without first realising the true relation between economics and political power. The disciples of Marx know well that both are connected — Marx himself said, " Power is an economic agency " — but they are unable to understand the true nature of their connection. They either neglect to distinguish between the two and believe the distribution of power to be at bottom identical with that of wealth, or they consider that all political power must form part of the " ideological superstructure ". As we have already pointed out, the distinction between conditions of production and the ideological superstructure is purely theoretical and does not correspond to anything

[1] Some English writers having said in defence of the expulsion of the yeomen that the depopulation of the country had served to increase the wealth of the nation, Marx accuses them of " hypocrisy ". I am, however, afraid that it was not hypocrisy, but the unfortunate tendency to esteem the means above the end, man's possessions and commodities above man himself, which is at the root of all our misery.

that exists in reality. The Marxists in general treat the ideological superstructure as a kind of dustbin, into which they throw legal conditions, political power, religion, philosophy and art, and many other things; in short, all that is not strictly economic or social. The distinction, moreover, is imaginary, and possible only in words.

Instead of examining facts and the causal connection between them, Marx proclaimed a series of dogmas, placing the productive forces at the root of everything, and declaring the conditions of production to be the sole essential reality, above which soars his " ideological superstructure " ; the latter being a curious conglomeration of institutions, laws, persons, works of art, books and God knows what, the most discordant category that was ever created by an abstract thinker, sitting at his desk, who had lost all touch with reality. For, whereas of the manifold phenomena included in the superstructure you may call opinions, science, poetry, philosophy and religion mere " reflections in the brain " if you like, it is impossible to class armies, governments, churches, law courts, etc., under the same head. Why should an army, as an instrument of politics, or a church with the congregation in it, a university, a theatre, or the pictures in a museum, the books in a library, be less real than manufacture of commodities or the rates of wages ? Moreover, are the social phenomena not very often at the same time political phenomena ? That economics are altogether dependent on thought, science and opinions, has been shown before. If a Marxist should object : Marx did not mean it like that, we should reply : if he did not mean it, why on earth did he say so ? Whereupon he would probably proceed to explain that Marx only intended to convey that the forms which armies governments, churches and universities take are determined by the conditions of production. That, even if we accept this interpretation, it is no more than a gratuitous assertion has been shown. Moreover, though it sounds logical, it is far from being logical. Is it possible to believe for a moment that government, armies, wars, religion and laws, science and opinions should have so much less influence on economic conditions than agriculture, manufacture and wages have on the former? Life shows the contrary every day. How can any phenomenon in this world be precluded from having effects to infinity? How can any link be broken out of the chain of infinite causality?

We can but repeat: the conditions of production are as much influenced and determined by the different elements of the superstructure, as these are by the economic basis. In fact, the so-called superstructure is itself quite as much the basis of production and of the conditions of production as the latter are its basis. In Marx's theory the true relation between the phenomena of life and history is obscured and distorted. Marxist historiography does not care for facts; it has no use for induction; it is entirely deductive. It does not trouble to investigate the causal connection of facts, which is always assumed beforehand; it does not even trouble to examine the chronological order of events. The conditions of production are the cause, once for all, and the rest follows. If the facts are not in accordance with the theory, so much the worse for the facts. They can, besides, always be arranged so as to suit the theory. Consequently, Marxist historiography is, on the whole, a falsification of history, though committed unconsciously and in good faith. Though it has to a large extent furthered economic research, it has been a check on the understanding of history and causes historical research to stray into a blind alley that leads nowhere.[1]

[1] Benedetto Croce who treats the Materialist Conception of History with gentleness, partly from respect for the important part which Marx's work and his endeavours fulfilled in the history of our time, says repeatedly that this conception is neither a new philosophy of history nor a new method of thought applied to history, but is merely an exhortation to pay more attention to the economic basis in order better to understand the historical developments. Cf. Benedetto Croce, *Il Materialismo Storico e l' Economia Marxista* (Bari, 1910), p. 70.

If this were the case, nobody would object. Friedrich Engels said, in fact, in the letter quoted on page 104, that " Marx and he had in their polemics sometimes exaggerated their assertions. They never imagined they were putting forth a formula by which all historical events could be explained ; if this were possible, the comprehension of a historical period would be as easy as the solution of a simple equation." These are indeed very reasonable words ; it is even possible that, being a man of different moods and of no solid foundations as a thinker, Engels really thought so for a moment. Unfortunately the numerous passages from Marx's and Engels' works, quoted in this study, reveal a very different opinion. And even if Marx and Engels had confined their theory within such reasonable bounds, these have long been overstepped in the system which their adherents have erected upon the basis of their theory. Countless laymen and not a few historians and sociologists do indeed believe that Marx's formula offers them a clue to the perfect understanding of all history. There are no longer any secrets for them. Mr. John Strachey says : " The materialist conception of history marks such an immense advance on any previous historical conception that to-day many people more or less unconsciously adopt its general standpoint. . . . The simplest thing to say on the materialist conception of history is that it reveals hitherto unperceived inter-connections between historical events . . ." (*op. cit.* pp. 358-9). The American sociologist Maurice Parmelee says in a recently published book, *Bolshevism, Fascism, and the Democratic State*, New York, 1934, on p. 49 : " The Marxists endeavour to dig down to the roots of the economic processes which are the principal if not the sole causal factors in history and social evolution ". The same author assured me that the number of historians who are of this opinion is constantly increasing.

CHAPTER V

THE HISTORICAL EPOCHS ACCORDING TO MARX

THERE follow two propositions, noteworthy because they offer evidence of how exclusively Marx, in formulating his theory, was influenced by the events of his own time.

These are propositions 11 : " No form of society can perish before all the forces of production which it is large enough to contain, are developed, and at no time will outworn conditions be replaced by new higher conditions as long as the material necessities for their existence have not been hatched in the womb of the old society itself ", and 12 : " Mankind never sets itself a problem that it cannot solve. At close examination it will always be found that no social problem ever arises unless the material conditions which make its solution possible, are either already in existence or at least developing."

While drawing up these sentences Marx certainly had in mind the fact that the new productive forces, steam and electricity, were already known when the French Revolution broke out, and manufacture by machinery was beginning to develop. In the same way, he saw in the political organisation of a large working class and in the enormous technical progress in the nineteenth century, the productive forces and the material conditions of existence needed for the future order of society which is to be the next stage of historical evolution. From this he concluded that the material conditions for the solution of new social problems are already in existence whenever mankind begins to think of their solution.

These propositions are open to a twofold criticism. In the first place, we must repeat what has been said in the first chapter, namely, that the *material* conditions for the solution of any human problem, the solution of which is at all possible, are in existence at all times. Steam and electricity existed before man appeared on earth. Only the *intellectual* feat of their discovery and the intellectual qualities necessary to produce it were still missing. All Marx's speculation is fatally vitiated by his fundamental mistake, which is to discard intellect in history as much as possible.

But setting aside this objection for the present and assuming that by " being in existence " Marx meant " being discovered or invented by human intellect ", we shall have to make a second objection. What Marx believes to be a universal truth, may be said to be true, at least in the main outlines, of the development during the last two hundred years, though some details would have to be examined more closely. Whether the future development and the great revolution expected by Marx will proceed along the same lines is an open question.[1]

[1] Even socialist and communist authors agree that the country in which the first socialist system of production is carried into effect on a large scale, Russia, was by no means economically the most advanced society nor the one best prepared for such an experiment. Mr. John Strachey, in his book quoted above, repeats over and over again how much easier and more successful a similar experiment would have been in Great Britain or in the United States of America, because their economic system is so much more advanced and developed. Marxist ideology in producing the Russian experiment acted regardless of Marxist theories.

Prophecies which as yet are not confirmed by events, may sometimes be profitable in politics, but are of no use whatever in science.

So much, however, is certain, the law which Marx thought he was stating, is not confirmed by the development in former recorded periods of history. It will, therefore, be opportune to consider the twelfth proposition in conjunction with the two preceding sentences. It runs as follows : " In bold outlines we may distinguish the Asiatic, the Antique, the Feudal and the modern Capitalist form of production, as progressive economic forms of society ". Thus are enumerated " in bold outlines " the successive periods in the evolution of society, which, according to Marx, were each prepared in the manner described in propositions 10 and 11, and brought about by revolutions as delineated in propositions 5 and 6. That is to say, each of these periods began when " at a certain stage of their development, the productive forces came into conflict with the existing conditions of production or — this is but a juristic expression for the same fact — with the existing conditions of property " because " from forms of development of the productive forces, the conditions of production had turned into fetters of these forces ".

It would be difficult to find a more unfortunate way of expressing the same idea than that chosen by Marx. To call the conditions of production forms of development of the productive forces, is as logical as to call warfare a form of development of arms, or tea-parties a form of development of tea. The conditions of production are forms of development, not of the productive forces, but of men's activity to satisfy their needs, an activity in which men make use of the productive forces ;

that is to say, they are forms of the use of the productive forces. The two modes of expressing the matter differ *toto coelo*. No less objectionable is the expression that the conditions of production turn into fetters of the productive forces. The conditions of production may at times prove an obstacle to the use of certain productive forces or to their being used in a certain manner. If anybody should reply that this is exactly what Marx meant, we should find the method of expression all the more deplorable. For in this place, as in some of the preceding propositions, he might, by a more correct and matter-of-fact way of expressing his thought, have preserved his followers from countless errors.

It may correctly be said that the conditions of production are apt to become fetters, not of the productive forces, but of *production*, just as institutions which have been founded with the object of promoting science, sometimes have turned into fetters of new research, and as religious organisations have sometimes turned into fetters of true piety. The reason of this is to be found in the inertia inherent to man's nature which makes him generally averse to innovations and to the introduction of new forms of any kind. Braunthal mentions this inertia, without pursuing the matter any further, though this conservative tendency in man is one of the most important factors in history, and moreover, a reality, not a mere form of speech like the " conflict between the productive forces and the conditions of production ". We shall therefore have to go into it, to a certain extent.

In the social life of men it has, owing to the egoism and the passions of the single individuals and to the controversies and other difficulties caused by them, at all times been indispensable to make certain rules and regulations destined to coerce this egoism and these passions. This has been as necessary in primitive times as it is in modern society. It is immaterial whether these rules are established by general consent or forced upon the community by some powerful person or group ; it is further immaterial whether they are known and sanctioned by tradition and habit or whether they be written laws. These rules, customs, traditions, laws, orders, whatever they may be called and however they may have come into existence, will always be a compound result of the need of the moment, on one hand, and the degree of insight possessed by those who impose them or agree on them, on the other. They may, therefore, be wisely made and useful, or foolish and obnoxious. They may be useful and expedient in some cases and prove useless or injurious in others, especially in some new and unforeseen situation. They may be advantageous for a part of the community or a class of society and disadvantageous for another. The distribution of power, from whatever source it may be derived, the superior bodily strength of a chieftain, or the military organisation commanded by the representatives of a certain class, will decide their introduction as well as the manner in which they are interpreted and applied. Now, it is in the interest of the community, or at least of a large or of the most powerful portion of it, that these rules, laws, customs or forms be maintained and observed, and penalties for their transgression are introduced. And even though in many cases there are no special sanctions, yet the accustomed and traditional forms have in all spheres of life, owing to men's inertia, such power over their souls that any deviation from them encounters serious difficulties. There is, however, an opposite tendency in men's souls, a wish for something new, a desire of change and innovation which is, as a rule, particularly strong in original and gifted individuals. The laws or rules being often inadequate or defective, people began to criticise them whenever injurious consequences were felt affecting individuals or groups or a whole class. Often different views finally got the upper hand, and the laws and customs were changed accordingly. Sometimes the change was gradual, sometimes it was brought about forcibly by a revolution. Thus, by the influx of ever new ideas, by criticising the established order till opinions and habits were changed, the intellectual and political life of the community developed, continuously restricted by those who desired to preserve what was traditional, as against those who wanted change. In the economic sphere new forces of production were discovered, or people tried to use the old well-known forces in a new and more profitable way, or the issue might be that other groups or another class demanded a share in the produce or the profits.

In this way there arise in every community controversies and disputes between those who desire to maintain the existing order of things, and those who want to change it. They arise not only in the economic sphere, but in all possible spheres of life, sometimes quite independently of each other, while sometimes the disputes in the different spheres are inter-connected. In any sphere of life it may happen that an order which for a while had been in force to general satisfaction, will delay the introduction of a new and better order. The old Prussian army regulations which had worked to perfection at the time of Frederick the Great, were a dead-weight on the Prussian infantry in 1806, when the close ranks proved an excellent target for the French, who fought in extended order ; and after the battle of Jena they had to be replaced by more modern regulations. The process is exactly the same in economic production. There is no mystical " development of the productive forces " ; they are discovered, tried, put to use, and whenever people discover new forces or new methods of employing the old, and expect better results and higher profits from the new ways, they will try to introduce them, whereas other people whose interests are different or who are unable to see the advantages of the new methods, will oppose them. That is all. Everybody knew this ; and only by the abstract form which Marx gave it, the mysterious formula declaring that the " development of the productive forces " and the " transformation of the conditions of production into fetters of these forces " were at the root of all historical revolutions, struck people as something extremely intelligent and new. In fact, high-sounding abstract words were put in lieu of the simple and concrete ; in the same way that a man might speak of an " apparatus to ward off the precipitations of the atmosphere " meaning an umbrella. The formulation, however, was not only euphuistic, but one-sided and in so far misleading. To Marx's theory of history one might, with a slight change, apply a saying of Lessing's : " This theory contains new and true statements ; but those statements which are true are not usually new, and those which are new are not usually true ".

The development described above is sometimes a slow one and sometimes accelerated ; whereas some races, and even whole continents, seem to be in a state of stagnation for long spaces of time, others seem to make comparatively rapid strides, and at certain moments in history the changes are so quick and violent as to appear catastrophical and are then called revolutions. It would, however, be false to assume that quick and violent changes that have far-reaching consequences are brought about solely in the way described and by the causes mentioned in Marx's fifth proposition. Great historical changes may arise from the most various origins, and not only from the circumstance that the conditions of production at a certain moment turned out to fetter, not the productive forces, but production. And even in those frequent cases in which economic reasons are the chief or partial source of a revolution, the process is not as simple as it is represented to be in Marx's propositions.

The greatest and most complete change in European history that is known to us, is the downfall of the Roman Empire, the destruction of antique civilisation, and the rise of feudalism and the feudal states in its place. Before we proceed to investigate this greatest catastrophe in our past, however, it seems advisable to look at the curious division of history into " progressive epochs " given in proposition 12. This division is so arbitrary and at the same time so perfunctory, so unfounded on the facts of historical evolution, as to confirm the supposition that Marx's knowledge of the early history of Europe and of mankind in general was very scanty, unless one assumes that the whole sentence was written in haste and without mature consideration. To be sure, historical science was not in 1859 what it is to-day ; in the eighty years which have passed since Marx wrote that unlucky sentence, researches of historians have extended the store of knowledge to an extraordinary degree; three thousand years have been, as it were, uncovered from under the sands of oblivion which had hidden them from memory. Yet even in 1859 historical science was not so far behind as to permit a division of this kind; besides, Marx lived full twenty-four years longer and might have retracted or altered it. Even his adherents do not seem to attach any value to this division; in the two volumes which Cunow devoted to expounding the theory, it is passed over in silence, nor does Labriola ever mention it.

What, for instance, does " Asiatic mode of production " mean ? Several thousand years before Christ, cities had been built in Mesopotamia, the capitals of kingdoms with a highly developed civilisation, while around their borders wild nomads wandered through more or less deserted regions. In the vast plains and in the mountainous tracts of India and of China, various races traversed all the stages of development from primitive hunting and cattle-breeding up to the erection of beautiful towns and civilised life. Nearly all of the different modes of production that existed before our time, succeeded each other, or were to be found simultaneously, in ancient Asia. We can only surmise that Marx was summing-up all the real or supposed modes of production and of social conditions that existed in early times, under the head " Asiatic ", because he knew little or nothing whatever about them. Though anybody is free to choose names and terms at will, it is advisable to choose scientific terms so as to designate something definite and not the most incongruous objects. Nor, even in framing a division in bold outlines, is it conceded to a historian or philosopher entirely to neglect the distinctive characteristics which are the foundations of the division.[1]

The term " antique mode of production " is just as meaningless. When and where did the antique mode of production begin replacing the Asiatic mode, and what on earth is the difference between the two ? In that part of the world which was the scene of antique civilisation, there lived tribes in a primitive state, there lived the farmers and warriors of the heroic age, there arose the Minoan civilisation, and later there existed simultaneously with the refined culture, the art and science and the complex political systems of Greece, the commercial republics of the Phoenicians and Carthaginians, and the Persian Empire with its half-nomadic, half-feudal nobility and with its tributary nations in the most varied stages of development. After its downfall, this Empire was divided into the cultivated Hellenistic kingdoms, while in the west there were the Italian peasant republics, one of which, owing to the military and political gifts of its people, in the course of a few centuries developed the highest political and economic system that existed before our time and in many points resembled the system which is in force at present. The term " antique mode of production ", far from designating a certain mode of production, includes the most varied economic systems. Some people might be inclined to accept as a common characteristic of antique

[1] Marx wrote in a very different fashion on periods and events with which he was familiar ; his description in *Capital* of the development of production from handicraft to manufacture and to capitalistic forms, a subject with which he was conversant as few others were, is incomparable, even though it may be, as Mantoux points out, too schematized in certain parts. Mantoux, *op. cit.* p. 71. An eminent German economist once said to the author of this study : " Without Karl Marx we should be unable to understand a good part of our economic development and of our situation ".

production that it was chiefly done by slave labour. This, however, is a feature which it has in common with the Asiatic mode of production and with that of many modern colonial states ; and then in the later ages of the Roman Empire, slave labour played a very subordinate part, because slaves were scarce.

It is only when he approaches more recent times that Marx gains a solid footing : one may safely distinguish between a feudal or mediaeval and a modern capitalistic mode of production. His theory is based on his knowledge of mediaeval and modern history, with which he was much better acquainted, whereas he knew but little of all previous epochs, and therefore contented himself with classifying them under these two inappropriate and unwarranted headings.

It was a further mistake to call these four periods progressive periods. Setting aside the fact that the historical evolution in the Far East, in a great part of Africa, and in the New World took a very different course, we shall have to make reservations even for that section of general history which Marx had in mind. Confining our research and our conclusions to European history, in which we must include that of Northern Africa and of the Near East as being inseparably connected with Europe and affected by the same movements and the same catastrophes, we may, basing our estimate on the growing command of the productive forces and on the increasing differentiation in all spheres of life, establish the fact of a progressive development from primitive life to the resplendent civilisation of ancient Rome and Greece. The political development from the wandering tribes of an early period to agriculture, to the building of great cities, to the foundation of republics and empires, as well as the economic development from barter to the elaborate monetary system and the world-embracing trade of later Antiquity, seems to proceed on an ascending slope. The transition, however, from Antiquity to the system which Marx calls the feudal system, is certainly no progress but rather a retrograde movement. Mankind sinks back towards a more primitive state ; in his political organisation man returns almost to nomadic and patriarchal times ; his economic system is no longer monetary but once more what is called natural economy. Then, after a long interval of barbarism, a new ascent begins, which is in many respects analogous to that of the past. Owing to the fact, however, that the remnants from the achievements of the antique world were of immeasurable value for the reconstruction of society, the ascent was much more rapid and a level was reached which was in many respects much higher.

Learning has taken great pains to find out the causes of that greatest and most fatal of all historical catastrophes, the fall of ancient Rome. It was formerly ascribed to the great migration of peoples, the wild German tribes being pressed westward and southward by Slavs and Mongols into the territory of the Empire, which they conquered and destroyed. This was a rather superficial view and one which did not afford much insight into the connection of events. The migration of peoples had begun many centuries earlier and lasted much longer ; one might perhaps say that it began with the dawn of mankind and has been going on ever since. Yet whenever, during previous centuries, the barbarians attempted to invade the Empire, they were defeated and repelled by the Roman legions. From the middle of the third century, however, and again in the fourth and after, the German invasions were constantly more successful, and finally Goths, Vandals, Franks conquered the western half of the Empire and divided it up. Clearly a change had come over the Empire itself, and it was soon understood that the reasons for this change had to be looked for in developments within the antique world. People used to speak of the Roman Empire's decay; decay, however, is a word that explains nothing; it states the deterioration but does not account for it. Neither does a reference to the so-called " law " according to which all living things, cities and empires among them, have their appointed time of growth, reach a culminating point and then begin to decline, get us any further; the spaces of time corresponding to each period are much too uncertain and variable. Some Empires and cities lasted several thousand years; others fell and disappeared after a few seasons. Some rose and declined and again became flourishing; in fact, no such law as the aforesaid can be discerned. Though the work of research to which students of all nations have devoted themselves during the last century, affords an insight into the story of the internal developments and the social and moral changes in the Roman Empire such as was not given to former generations, historians and sociologists have not by any means arrived at the same conclusion. Many of them have laid the blame on the emperors under whose despotic rule the virile qualities and the independent spirit of the Romans were stifled and became extinct. Though this is perfectly true, it does not explain why the Romans tolerated this despotic rule and did not rise against the emperors. As we now know, both Augustus and Tiberius made wise but vain endeavours to strengthen the authority of the Senate in order to create a counterpoise to their own power. Otto Seeck is of opinion that the extermination of the best men in the civil wars, by the proscriptions which followed them, and by the many executions ordered by suspicious emperors, unnerved the people and ruined the national character, the more so as it was invariably the fate of the most courageous and independent persons to fall under suspicion and be put to death. There may be a certain amount of truth in this, though it is probable that Seeck exaggerates the effect of this persecution. We know of too many countries and empires ruled by despotic princes in which every independent movement was suffocated, every free utterance forbidden, any person who incurred the displeasure of the government imprisoned, exiled or killed, and yet in each of these countries the people finally rose against their oppressors and dethroned them. Another cause, according to Seeck, was the depopulation of the Empire due to a false economic system. The very fact of depopulation is, however, a matter of dispute, and convincing arguments have been put forward against it. During about two hundred years the nations united in the Roman Empire enjoyed a period of nearly unbroken peace the like of which mankind has known neither before nor since. Only in the remotest frontier regions of the vast Empire, which extended from Britain in the north-west and Morocco in the south-east to Mesopotamia, were there occasional fights, perhaps a punitive expedition against some savage tribe, or the incorporation of some new stretch of border country ; in the interior of the Empire there was absolute peace. We know that all the countries of which it was composed were prosperous ; their wealth grew, and though population in antique times increased at a much slower rate than to-day, yet the number of the Empire's inhabitants must during two centuries have at least doubled.[1] Besides, whether this was the case or not, the population of the Roman Empire even at the time of its undoubted decay was so infinitely superior in numbers to the Germans — a hundred millions against savage tribes which, when most numerous, could raise perhaps some fifteen or twenty thousand armed men — that numbers cannot possibly have been the reason of Roman inferiority.[2] It is well known that the Romans, when threatened by Alaric, King of the Visigoths, boasted of their numbers, a boast confirmed by his scoffing answer: " The thicker the grass, the easier it is to mow it ". Max Weber, in his turn, traced back the economic decay to the fact that production in Antiquity was based almost exclusively on slave labour. He is of opinion that in the inland regions of the Empire, where there was not much traffic, production had for its principal object the supplying of the landowners' and householders' own needs, whereas trade, being chiefly ocean trade, transported " a thin layer of very valuable commodities for the use of a thin layer of rich people ". " The slave-owner ", says Weber, " represented the economic basis of antique civilisation ", and when, under the emperors, wars ceased to be frequent and the supply

[1] Otto Seeck, *Geschichte des Untergangs der antiken Welt* (Berlin, 1910), vol. i. pp. 270 *sqq.*, 338 *sqq.* Beloch computes the population of the Roman Empire at 54 millions at the time of the death of Augustus in the year A.D. 14. This total is the result of very conservative calculations. See K. J. Beloch, *Die Bevölkerung der griechisch-römischen Welt* (Leipzig, 1896), p. 507.

[2] Hans Delbrück, *Geschichte der Kriegskunst im Rahmen der politischen Geschichte*, vol. ii., " Die Germanen " (3rd ed. Berlin, 1921), pp. 3, 233 *sqq.*, 300 *sqq.*

of slaves was stopped in consequence, production began
to decline. Soon a lack of working hands made itself
felt, which became so acute that the owners of the large
estates in Italy began to kidnap wanderers and travellers
on solitary roads, and the emperors saw themselves
compelled to issue several decrees against this crying
abuse. As no slaves could be found, agriculture devolved
upon half-free serfs, the so-called *coloni*, who did compulsory labour. Trade dried up, the cities fell into ruin.[1]
When we consider that beside all these calamities there
was a growing scarcity of precious metals, and if we add
to these economic circumstances the pernicious effects
of a wrong distribution of power, we must ascribe great
importance to these changes.

Other authors see the cause in the mixture of races
and the deterioration of the ruling race by intermarriages
with slaves and freedmen. Intermixture was encouraged
by the extension of civil rights to all the inhabitants of
the Empire, and there may be some truth in the opinion
that the consequences for the quality of the Roman race
were not always desirable ; in particular, admixture
with some Oriental races may have made the Romans
more willing to submit to despotic rule. It must, however, be taken into consideration that the blood of some
very warlike and independent races like the Celts, the
Germans, the Jews and the Arabs, was mingled with
that of the Italian race. Vilfredo Pareto holds the
opinion that the growing rigidity and uniformity of
thoughts and customs, the " ossification " of all institutions and the bad " circulation of the élites " due to this
rigidity, was the essential cause of the decline and fall.

---

[1] Max Weber, " Die sozialen Gründe des Untergangs der antiken Welt ",
in *Die Wahrheit* (Stuttgart, 1896), vol. 6, no. 3, pp. 457 *sqq.*

It seems probable that all these circumstances and changes, and perhaps some others unknown to us, combined to produce that disastrous result. Such is usually the case. It is generally a fatal error to look for a single factor as the cause of some great historical change. Social organisations are very complex entities which are constantly exposed to the action and influence of multiple agencies.

It has been previously pointed out that in order to understand any historical process it is all-important first to know how it took place. It is in most cases as interesting as it is difficult to find out what may be regarded as the first signs or symptoms of the movement in question — which in our case is the decline of the Roman Empire — and then to pursue the manifold phenomena betraying its progress until we reach the one that brings it to a definite termination. We shall then at least know exactly what happened and how the result, in our case the ruin, was accomplished.

There cannot be any doubt whatever that the fact by which the downfall of the Roman Empire was ultimately brought about, was the decay of its military power. In spite of their vast numbers, the Romans were unable to raise armies capable of taking the field against the Germans. There was again more than one reason for this. It cannot be denied that civilisation and a higher intellectual development makes men less perfect warriors. In a peaceful world this might be a matter of indifference ; in the world of men, however, as we know it to be, the fact is no unalloyed blessing, and may in certain cases prove to be disastrous. Civilisation, it is true, develops qualities which render men who are more nervous and sensitive than hardy and muscular savages, nevertheless superior to the latter. Human intelligence invented arms and a military art to which the bravest barbarian warriors must succumb. Though the disparity of armaments was in former times not nearly so great as it is now, yet owing to their highly developed tactics, perfect discipline, and an efficient commissariat, the Roman legions were victorious in all encounters with wild warriors.

Growing riches and a refined culture, however, along with the habits of a long peace, made the Roman citizens less and less inclined to submit to that hard and severe discipline and ever less minded to take service in the army. Neither did the proletarians of the capital, who were sustained by imperial donations of grain, who paid no taxes and passed their lives enjoying feasts and spectacles, feel any desire to become soldiers and endure the hardships of war. There were so many less civilised and very warlike nations at the disposal of the Roman government; Illyrians, Arabs, Germans above all, served in the armies. The emperors, ever distrustful of the Roman nobles, rather favoured this development. An economic factor supervened to subvert the military organisation. Until the second century before Christ the Roman armed forces had been a militia, the able-bodied citizens being called in when a war broke out. Conditions had changed, however, during the second Punic war. The militia was replaced by an army of professional soldiers, the prolonged, almost permanent, wars of the republic and the extension of its territory making this change inevitable. Under the emperors the army retained its professional character; the time when the Roman citizens could be called to arms was long past. In the third century, however, precious metals became scarce in the Roman Empire ; a constant exportation of gold in course of commerce had drained the funds, and the mines became more and more exhausted. Owing to this situation, the standard of coinage was continuously depreciated. It finally became impossible to pay the army regularly ; and the government resorted to the expedient of assigning land to the legionaries in garrison along the frontiers of the Empire. The troopers settled themselves and cultivated the allotted farms ; they were no longer real soldiers, but peasants under an obligation to fight in emergency cases. It was again a militia, but how different from the old Roman militia ! The constant drilling and practising ceased, the incomparable Roman discipline was soon lost, the tactics were forgotten. Yet, so gradual was the change that it was scarcely noticed ; the effects, however, soon made themselves felt. In the vast Empire there was no lack of able-bodied young men, but they showed no inclination to serve, nor were there enough officers and drill-sergeants to organise them. In this predicament the imperial government resorted to hiring entire barbarian tribes who engaged themselves to defend the Empire against other barbarians who should invade it. Very soon the so-called " Roman " armies which fought the German tribes beyond the frontiers, themselves consisted of German warriors who were paid for the service.[1]

German tribes in ever-increasing numbers were either called into the Empire or entered it of their own accord, offering to fight for it. It was inevitable that these men, who were the instrument and the support

[1] Hans Delbrück, *op. cit.* vol. ii. ch. 10, " Niedergang und Auflösung des römischen Kriegswesens ".

of other people's power, one day became conscious of this fact and finally apprehended the real state of things so that their leaders felt inclined to seize power for themselves. Opportunities were not wanting ; they might pick quarrels with the inhabitants, the chiefs might fall out with a Roman governor, or have grievances against the Emperor himself ; or the possessions of those whom they knew to be defenceless, might simply tempt their avidity. The defenders made themselves the masters, conquered the Empire, exterminated part of its inhabitants and subjugated the others. The barbarian nations who surrounded the Empire, Huns, Normans, Saracens, seeing the disorder and the helplessness, the possibilities of making the richest booty without running great risks, came one after the other, raiding the coasts and the great cities inland. Thus antique civilisation was stamped out. It is a phenomenon that repeats itself in history that a rich and civilised nation, lacking sufficient military power, will fall a prey to warlike and rapacious neighbours.

This certainly was the way in which the whole process was consummated ; the decline of military power and organisation was decisive, whatever the first origin and the following steps of general decay and deterioration may have been. The exploitation of the provinces, the mixture of races, the decomposition of the Roman people into an aristocracy abounding in wealth and a destitute lower class, the economic system based on large estates and production by slave labour to which the lack of slaves ensuing from a long period of unbroken peace proved fatal, the decay of the constitution and the extinction of all political life, the ossification of all institutions, with simultaneous lawlessness and constant troubles,

the exhaustion of the mines, the ruinous system of taxation under the later emperors, and the final disorganisa-
tion of the military force, all these co-operated in the
fatal concatenation and mutual interaction.

Although, as we have seen, economic and social
reasons did play an important part in the destruction of
the antique world, we can discover no trace of any new
development of the productive forces, or of their being
fettered by the conditions of production, having any
part in the catastrophe. No new productive forces were
put to use in these centuries ; on the contrary, a constant
decline of the existing forces of production is clearly
discernible. There is nothing visible but decay, followed
by invasion and destruction by the barbarians ; no
progressive evolution, but a relapse into a lower and
more primitive mode of production. It is a revolution
of a peculiar kind, very different from those earlier
revolutions and changes from cattle-breeding and primitive agriculture to higher economic and social systems,
as well as from later developments like the transition
to a monetary system of economy in the last centuries
of the Middle Ages, or that to machine-work and great
industry in modern times. There have, of course, been
numerous similar cases of inward decay and outward
destruction in history, though certainly on a much
smaller scale. Nature and history produce countless
forms and ever-new combinations and changes, and
they are not to be pressed into the patterns and formulas
which Marx thought he could impose.

No " progressive period " followed on the destruction of the antique world ; but the countries around the
Mediterranean relapsed into a more primitive state,
due to the radical destruction of the known productive

forces, as well as of the goods produced and of the existing conditions of production, and still more to the destruction of science and all intellectual culture.

Marx and his adherents choose to call the new period the feudal. One may employ this term, though Feudalism, properly so called, as a purely Germanic institution was confined to the Germanic states that formed a very small part of the known world. The great Byzantine Empire, by far the most civilised part of the mediaeval world, knew no Feudalism in the Western sense of the word; it was equally unknown in the Slav countries; it never played a part worth mentioning in Italy, while in England it was soon divested of its essential characteristics. True Feudalism existed only in France and Germany; from there it spread partly into the adjacent regions. It is not Feudalism that is characteristic of the mode of production in this period, but barter and payment in kind, what is called natural economy in contradistinction to the monetary system of economy. It was the same system of economy which had prevailed before the rise of antique civilisation and to which the European nations had returned. Feudalism, properly so called, was not an economic, but a military organisation. For purely military reasons, the land was assigned to prominent warriors who in their turn kept and drilled subordinate warriors; they were invested with it on condition that they should be ready to fight for their liege lord, attended by their warriors. Political power being always and everywhere dependent on military power, and particularly so in warrior states like these new Germanic kingdoms, the political system conformed to the military organisation or rather was, in fact, identical with it. That the land was not given to the great as an independent property, but was — probably in imitation of certain ecclesiastical customs — lent on condition of military assistance, was a political precaution, an attempt on the part of the ruler to retain the sovereign power secure in his hands, an attempt not generally crowned with success. The feudal system resulted from the imperfect economic system described above ; for no sooner was there enough money in a country than the kings hired and paid standing armies. It was, however, by no means a necessary consequence of the system ; barter and payment in kind existed throughout the world for ages, yet no Feudalism resulted from it. Feudalism was a singular phenomenon that prevailed for some time in certain parts of Europe. There existed similar institutions in the Persian Empire, in Japan and in the Aztec Empire in the New World. Similar conditions will sometimes, though by no means always, lead to the establishment of similar institutions. The institutions of a nation must necessarily be adapted to its economic conditions, but they do not of necessity result from them.

It has, however, become customary to call the period that of Feudalism, as contrasted with the modern system of economics which has since replaced it. Used in this sense, the word means the rule of great landed proprietors who generally form the nobility of the country and on whose estates live a greater or smaller number of tenants — regardless of the existence of fiefs and feudal duties. These existed in but a few countries in the Middle Ages and were to be found in antique Persia long before the beginning of the so-called feudal period.

Sterile and terrible as the first centuries of the new epoch were, the conditions of Europe were not unfavourable to a revival. The Germans were a gifted race ;

they were not only first-class fighters, but capable of political organisation and economic activity. The races which had of old inhabited the Empire, had lost their culture but not their talents. Moreover, important fragments of their civilisation had escaped destruction and survived the fall of the Empire. These were, in the first place, the Church, then a few municipal laws and institutions and a number of Latin and Greek manuscripts, which in course of time were discovered in the monasteries and read, the Church, which preserved the Latin language, providing the clue. Owing to these fortunate coincidences, the interval of barbarism did not this time endure for thousands of years, and the recovery was comparatively rapid. As a final result, European civilisation had moved northward. Whereas, in the days of Antiquity the southern and western countries of Europe had formed the northern part of the civilised world, they were now its southern limit, central and northern Europe having been added while northern Africa had been lost.

Catastrophes quite as ruinous as the destruction of the Western Empire by the Germans befell northern Africa and the Near East. The large civilised regions of northern Africa were devastated by the Arabs, those of Asia by ever repeated invasions of Mongol hordes. The wide stretches of nearly desert land, where once stood rich and flourishing cities, bear witness to the devastation which for centuries raged over these unhappy countries. The invaders had neither the talent nor the eagerness to learn of the Germanic races, and though a few gifted monarchs tried to make their courts centres of culture, new inroads soon destroyed such happy beginnings, and the whole region remained for centuries in a state which was more or less one of stagnation, until, in the nineteenth and twentieth centuries, European influences again caused a revolution of a peculiar kind.

In formulating his conception of history, Marx fell a victim to the delusions of historical perspective which magnifies the importance of the events and objects of a man's own time, whereas his insight into former epochs is dimmed by their remoteness. Impressed by the events and the revolutions which happened in his own time or in times not long past, he considered these alone and so was led to a false measure of time, to an untenable division of history, and to erroneous conclusions in general. The rise of modern capitalism was something so extraordinary and attended by consequences so far-reaching, that a man, and a good part of his generation with him, might be dazzled by it.

We are now in a position to see perfectly what is erroneous in the eleventh and the twelfth propositions. Very little is known to us of the fate and the extinction of the older forms of society. As for the early transitions from primitive hunting and fishing to cattle-breeding and primitive agriculture, or the transitions from one of the two last-named states to the other, all that we can say about them rests on assumptions and hypotheses. It is more than probable that countless primitive societies were destroyed and exterminated by war, by the invasion of foreign enemies, and we may conclude by analogy that the change from one form of society to another was often due to imitation or to foreign pressure. But we know nothing at all of the original progress of any ancient tribe or nation to a new mode of production and a new social organisation. No documents, no reports from those remote times have reached us, only legends and myths.

Now, what may be the meaning of the following sentence : " At no time will outworn conditions be replaced by new and higher ones, as long as the material pre-requisites necessary for their existence have not been hatched in the womb of the old society itself " ? Nothing, of course, can come into existence unless the conditions necessary for its existence are given, which is to say, nothing can exist if its existence is not possible. Yet many things do not come into existence, though their existence should seem possible. Marx says further : " No form of society can perish, before all the productive forces are developed which it is large enough to contain ". Who is to know and to decide what forces a given form of society is large enough to contain ? We have shown in our second chapter how productive forces are discovered and what are the conditions required for their being put to use. Why should it have been impossible for the ancient Romans to find a new technical method further to exploit their mines ? Or why should they not have been able to introduce payment by cheque or order, of which the rudiments already existed ? They did not lack the necessary energy, they were intelligent enough, their trade and their business life was highly organised ; natural science had begun ; the archetype of the steam-engine already existed : why should human civilisation, having once attained so high a level, not have gone on developing in a straight ascendant line ? The answer is obviously: because the Romans were surrounded by sturdy barbarians by whom their civilisation was destroyed and its further development prematurely cut short. There also was that mysterious process of decay within the Antique world by which the existing forces were paralysed and withered. But who can say that no revival, no reform, no resurrection would have taken place, the like of which has often happened in history, and that the Empire would not have begun to flourish in new vigour, had it not been for the barbarians ? All such questions are of course idle speculation. All that is, is necessary, and the fate of the Roman Empire could not have been different. But Marx's theory is incompetent to account for this fate ; prematurely advanced on the basis of certain events, it is — partially — true of these events only, and not of universal application.[1]

Marx says further : " Mankind never sets itself a problem which it cannot solve ". How are we to know which are the problems that mankind sets itself at the present moment or which it has set itself in the past ? Are we to infer them from men's desires, their longing for well-being, their dreams of a state in which justice will reign and everybody be happy and contented ? Or are we to see them in the questions put by science, the solution of which may be of the utmost importance for mankind ? Or, again, are they just the questions at issue at a certain time in a certain place ? In that case we should have to say that not only every age and every country but every group and every individual has to face different problems. Moreover, the fact that the greatest part of these problems were never solved and probably did not admit of a solution is so patent that we cannot suppose Marx to have had these problems in mind. He probably meant those great social changes,

[1] " The history of the world does not consist merely of class war ; the social philosophers of the nineteenth century felt the concern about the material well-being of the rising masses in Europe as the most urgent problem of the time, and applied it as a heuristic principle to former times", V. Valentin, *Weltgeschichte* (Amsterdam, 1939), vol. i. p. 11.

those revolutions of the entire social order which are treated by him in the preceding as well as in the following propositions. We have, however, seen that the problems which led to these changes, are manifold and complicated, and that the changes themselves, though in some cases they may be regarded as representing progress, just as often took the form of retrogression, decay and destruction. We have seen that they generally resulted from conflicting human passions, lust of power, ambition and greed, from unwise measures taken by governments or ruling classes, and in other cases from new discoveries and inventions. It is only in these last-mentioned cases that the development of the productive forces plays a part.

It is further clear that only in a few exceptional cases was any problem that society set itself, ever really solved ; and even then it was always only a partial and very imperfect solution, and one which in course of time developed into something unforeseen and often undesirable and, at any rate, a result quite different from what had been expected. For what is a " problem " or a " task " but an opinion in one man's head, or in several, that something should be done, that a certain change was desirable ? In what manner were the transitions made, from one " progressive period " to another, how did men pass from one state of production to the next ? When a hunting tribe had domesticated a few head of cattle, grazed the flock and bred some young cattle, they were ripe for nomadism ; and when they had learned to sow and reap the fruits of the earth, they were ripe for agriculture. When a few cunning persons began to trade and some intelligent people had the idea of weighing pieces of metal and using them for buying and selling, they were ripe for commerce and, in course of time, for a monetary system of economics. Thus the problem did arise, as Marx says, when the conditions which made its solution possible, were already in existence or at least developing. Yet this is only to say : nomadism, agriculture and money all appeared when they appeared ; a tautology which explains nothing, a paraphrase of the fact in different words. The countless cases in which the problems remained unsolved, the desired and most desirable ends were not reached, and no progress accomplished, the cases of nations which perished with all their civilisations like the Roman Empire, the Hellenistic and the Asiatic kingdoms, are not taken into consideration. I said they were not taken into consideration, because obviously Marx did not ignore all these events ; he only set them aside and failed to draw from them the inevitable conclusions which would have upset his theory. It was the fatal habit of arriving, by a purely mental process, at abstract statements which led Marx, who was quite capable in other cases of studying the concrete facts and drawing the necessary conclusions, into advancing those untenable generalisations.

In order to be in accordance with truth, that is, with the real course events took, the proposition would have to be worded as follows : it sometimes happens, in the course of history, that a tribe, a nation, or a group of nations, under certain circumstances, owing perhaps to a peculiar geographical position or to an exceptional political development, to the appearance in its midst of some great individual, to contact with a superior race — provided it is not exterminated by the latter — ensures its continued existence and further development by the discovery and use of new productive forces, and thus attains a higher level of civilisation and a more highly organised form of society. When such cases repeat themselves in the history of a nation or of a group of nations, they may in their succession be considered as " progressive " periods. In such cases the problems which mankind sets itself or which are set to it by circumstances, find a solution, though the word has to be understood in a metaphorical sense. In a great many cases, however, the problems are not solved and the evolution is cut short ; in other cases a stagnation takes place, which may last for centuries and more, until the favourable circumstances mentioned above present themselves and a new stage of development sets in.

The truth is that Marx, in formulating his propositions, took into consideration only the transition from mediaeval to modern times, and that from the social state prevailing in the eighteenth century to that in the nineteenth, that is, the transitions from natural to monetary economy, and from production by handicraft and manufacture on a small scale to great industries and international commerce. These are transitions to which his theory, if interpreted in a large sense and with important corrections, may be safely applied.

Marx took it for granted that the future transition to the new socialistic economy and to the socialistic and communistic form of society would be achieved in exactly the same fashion. Looking forward, he was optimistic and thought that the problem which he as labour leader put before the world, would find an adequate solution. Looking backward, he disposed lightly of thousands of years, overlooked the destruction of entire civilisations, and so was able to establish the existence of a succession of progressive periods. In writing these sentences, he was influenced by a political idea, rather than by scientific reasoning.

The last two propositions serve to corroborate this opinion. They are (proposition 14) : " The present capitalistic conditions of production are to be considered as the last antagonistic form of society, not in the sense of individual antagonism, the antagonism rather takes its origin from the social conditions of life of the individuals. The productive forces, however, which are developing under the present system, are at the same time creating the material conditions which will make possible the solution of this antagonism." (15) : " This social system is, therefore, the closing phase of the pre-history of human society ".

After having in an arbitrary way constructed the history of the past, Marx feels equal to the task of delineating the history of the future. The antagonism resulting from the social conditions of the individuals is class war, of which there has been no question in the propositions until now ; it is, however, sufficiently discussed in Marx's other writings. This antagonism, this class war, is to cease completely after the coming revolution. The new productive forces growing in the womb of existing society will make this possible. However, the theory revealed in the first thirteen propositions did not lead us to expect this result ; no reason is given why the productive forces developed in our own time should have this effect announced in the fourteenth proposition. This conclusion stands in no logical connection whatever with the preceding argument. The explanation is given in other writings. " The greatest of all productive forces ", says Marx in *The Poverty of Philosophy*,

" is the revolutionary working-class itself." The material conditions for the end of class antagonism are to be seen in the fact that the enormous quantity of goods produced by modern technique would, if only the distribution were different, suffice to satisfy the needs of all and to satiate those who are now suffering from hunger. If Marx had inserted this sentence in his propositions, the logical gap would have been filled.

It is easy enough to confute what Marx says of past history ; · whereas no one is in a position to confute his construction of the history of the future. It is as impossible to confute as to prove. It is a prophecy and, being such, shares the nature of all prophecies : it may come true or it may not. And if a man who believes he knows the future history of mankind, declares all history up to the present time to be only the " pre-history ", he is free to do so. By doing so, he introduces, consciously or not, a moral element into his theory of history, an appraisement of all that is behind us ; all that has been done and achieved up to the time of that future revolution, is declared to be only a preparatory stage of less perfection than the coming perfect state of society. As Marx, however, is averse to moral points of view, he cannot openly favour what he condemns, and so he introduces his moral judgments in the disguise of a pretended law that is to bring about of necessity that state which he considers just and desirable.

We pointed out above that this " law " does not necessarily result from Marx's theory. From his description of the process of historical evolution, it does not follow that the coming revolution must of necessity produce a state without classes, still less that such a state would be a permanent one. We have not the faintest notion what productive forces the human mind may discover in the course of the coming centuries and millenniums, and what use our descendants will make of them. We do not know — unfortunately — whether a more just and equal distribution of wealth will result from future revolutions, nor whether and what future discoveries will lead to eternal peace, whereas all former gave origin to strife and discord. Such a hope may be an Utopia, or it may, perchance, come true ; but, in either case, it has nothing to do with history.

Another passage of the work quoted above may serve to explain why Marx did not find it necessary logically to demonstrate the contents of the fourteenth proposition. He says : " As history proceeds and the struggle of the proletariat becomes ever more clearly defined, they " — that is, the theorists of the working classes, socialist and communist writers — " no longer need to look for science in their brains. They need only observe and consider what is occurring under their very eyes and make themselves the instrument of the movement which they see." It is of no use to oppose scientific arguments to a man who is conscious of understanding the present and of seeing the future. We are no longer in the sphere of science, but in that of politics. Now, all political activity being an attempt to influence the future course of history, a man who desires to do this, may have good reasons for asserting that he knows the future, and if he is con-vinced of this, so much the better for him ; for he will be able to speak and to act with so much more assurance and unhampered by any doubt.

We said that the subject of class war, the last stage of which, according to what is said in the 14th proposi-tion, has now begun, is treated in other works. The theory of class war is explicitly set forth in the *Communist Manifesto*. While the productive forces are considered to be the basic element in history, and the conditions of production as a form of development of these forces, whereas all the rest is nothing but an ideological superstructure and, as such, a consequence of the conditions of production, class war is the method or the form in which the historical evolution of mankind is accomplished. We read in the first paragraph of the *Communist Manifesto*: " The history of all societies that existed up to our time, is the history of class struggles ; free men and slaves, patricians and plebeians, barons and serfs, masters and companions of a guild, in short, oppressors and oppressed, lived in constant opposition to one another, and in uninterrupted warfare against one another, a war which at certain times was latent and at other times became open strife, and which every time ended either in a revolutionary transformation of the whole society or in the extinction of both classes ".

We do indeed find class struggles or at least class differences in nearly all countries and times since civilisation began. It was Plato who wrote, " There are two states in the state, one is that of the rich, the other that of the poor ". In Athens and in Rome class struggles went on for centuries. They play a conspicuous part in all mediaeval countries and towns as well as in modern times ; and now, at present, since the classes have become conscious of the struggle and since there exists a theory of it, it plays an even greater part than ever before.

Nevertheless, the way in which history is declared to be merely a record of class struggles, is open to objection. In the German original it is said, " the history of all forms of society up to our own time is the history of class struggles ", and Cunow says in comment upon this sentence, " that until now class struggles have played the most important part in social evolution and that all political life bears the stamp of it ",[1] which is putting it in a less exclusive manner ; yet in the French translation the wording is as follows, " L'histoire de toute société jusqu'à nos jours n'a été que l'histoire des luttes de classe ", that is, " has been nothing but the history of class struggles ". It is this idea which has been generally accepted and which we find expressed everywhere in Marxist historiography.

However great the importance of class struggles may have been, their influence was by no means the only one that shaped society, and it cannot even be said that they are the most important fact in history, unless seen from a class standpoint. He who studies history with an unbiased mind, will find that wars between nations certainly played no less a part. We may even say that, as a rule, they were more frequent, more violent, caused much more bloodshed and were certainly more effective in deciding the fate and the development of the peoples of the earth than domestic struggles. The farther back we trace the history of mankind, to times in which there was no uniform civilisation, when men were much more divided than they are to-day, and the difference between them much more accentuated, in those times each tribe, each nation, each town was the other's declared enemy, and they stood over against each other in serried ranks. Even in our time, the national feeling, the consciousness of belonging to the same country, proves in foreign wars, with very few exceptions, to be stronger than all class differences. All through history ruling classes and

[1] Cunow, *op. cit.* vol. ii. p. 77.

subject classes, rich and poor, fought as co-nationals side by side against foreign enemies. It is immaterial whether the reason was an " antiquated ideology ", a " lack of class consciousness ", the " suggestion of patriotism ", or a natural feeling of belonging to those to whom they were bound by the same blood, the same language, and many common interests. The fact has been demonstrated in the past and, as the Great War and many wars since have shown, it is the same at present. It is quite possible that with the spread of a different ideology there will be a change in this respect, but until now it has certainly been so.

It is a curious fact that in the fifteen propositions regarded as the " classical formulation " of Marx's theory of history, war, the phenomenon which throughout history has had the most fatal consequences and brought about the most important changes, and which decides in the last resort even inner struggles and revolutions, is not even mentioned.[1] When one asks a Marxist for his views on war, he will invariably answer that war is the inevitable consequence of capitalism. Capitalists need constant new markets for production,

[1] In the draft mentioned on p. ii we find the following passage : " War was developed before peace. It has to be shown that certain economic phenomena such as hired labour, engines, etc., are developed by war and in the armies before they appear in the domestic sphere." This sentence proves that Marx was aware that economic facts may be determined by war ; it gives, however, no clue as to what Marx considered to be the part and the importance of war in his theory of history. In the *German Ideology* it is said on page 12, concerning some remarks on the development of townships : " The fact of conquest seems to contradict this conception of history " ; thereupon follow a few sentences on the destruction of the Roman Empire by the barbarians, which, however, also fail to provide a clue. Engels has written pamphlets and articles on military questions, and in an Appendix to his *Anti-Dühring* he attempts to prove that military power as well as the methods of military art are entirely dependent on the economic development.

the nations compete for these markets, and in the long run these economic tensions force governments and nations into war.

Now, capitalism has existed for a few centuries, whereas wars have been fought for many thousands of years ; indeed, we know of no period of history in which there have been no wars. Who, then, and what caused the wars before capitalism came into existence ? — The only Marxist state which exists, and which boasts of being constituted according to the theories of Marx, Soviet Russia, made war on Poland almost as soon as it was constituted. It was a foreign war which was lost and therefore has not yet been repeated. But the Russian state has armaments and the largest standing army in the world. Possibly this army is kept for the sole purpose of defence against foreign aggression ; so much is nevertheless sure, that even when capitalism has been replaced by communism, war does not cease on that account. Thus we find war before capitalism, under capitalism and after capitalism. The conclusion is obvious and inevitable : as the most different conditions of production lead to war or, let us rather put it this way, as we find war compatible with the most different systems of political economy, these systems of economy cannot possibly be the true cause of war ; there must be another reason for it independent of economics. If an illness is apt to befall patients before the time of puberty, during this time, and after it, puberty cannot be its sole cause. The truth is : men make war because they are a disputatious and rapacious race ; prone to violence by nature, whenever they meet with any opposition to their wishes or to their passions and even to their opinions ; and, as long as they do not mend their ways and get rid of these qualities, there will be wars under any social system. A communist state will, if it feels strong enough, certainly make war on other states in order to destroy capitalism, and it is more than probable that even if communism were the ruling system in all countries of the world, dissensions would arise on the way in which the system is to be carried into effect, different ideas as to the true nature of communism would create discord among parties and, the difference of races contributing to widen the gulf, different opinions and interests would soon lead to armed strife. Being a question of the future, we can but say, this result is very probable, no more.

We do not think that Marx himself considered war as being the fruit of capitalism. Yet we are at a loss to say where in his system he assigned a place to this terrible phenomenon. Did he include it in the ideological super-structure as he did politics and institutions? Or is it, perhaps, a productive force? No doubt many tribes lived on war; nations like the Romans grew rich and powerful chiefly by war. Nevertheless it does not seem possible that Marx would have included it under this head. All these are not merely vain questions. They prove how one-sided were the views of the founders of the theory, and how carelessly they left out of considera-tion whatever did not of itself, so to speak, fall in with their first thoughts. It seems strangely illogical to make internal struggles the basis of all development and to treat foreign wars perfunctorily and incidentally when they happen to be in question. Marx and his followers are, for moral and political reasons, principally interested in social questions and problems. Absorbed in them, they gave no heed to many other phenomena, or threw them into the great melting-pot of the ideological super-structure ; and it seems they disposed of war in the same way.

Up to our time, foreign wars had a more decisive influence on the destinies of nations and of mankind than all class wars, perhaps the French Revolution alone excepted. It was war that destroyed the civilisation which mankind had attained in Antiquity and hurled Europe back into barbarism. It was war that devastated great parts of Asia and prevented any wholesome civil development. Whatever misery has been caused by the oppression and exploitation of one class by the other, it is not to be compared to the horrors and to the fatal consequences which foreign wars have brought upon mankind. It is true that civil wars may be still more or at least quite as terrible ; but then, civil wars are by no means always due to class differences, whereas foreign wars have ever and again united hostile classes in defence against a foreign foe. The classes have many times been divided in themselves by party struggles which caused members of different classes, high and low, to fight together against the opposing party. Vassals, serfs, citizens, masters and men fought at the side of the nobles of their party in the age-long wars of the Guelphs and the Ghibellines in Italy, which were caused partly by the discordant interests of the cities and the Emperor, and by clerical and national interests, and partly by local feuds. Conditions in the real world are usually much too complex to make possible a division of classes in two clearly defined front lines. While it is true that the largest Italian cities and those allied to them fought for the burghers' independence of imperial government, other townships took the Emperor's side from pure hatred of the cities that were arrayed against him. Pisa and Siena were Ghibelline for no other reason than that Florence was Guelph. Those who were opposed to the Emperor, were allied with France or other princes or with the Pope, and the entire Italian nobility was divided against itself. And while in every Italian town there were continuous dissensions between the nobility and the burghers, and again between the guilds and the common people, the "plebe minuta",—dissensions which often led to fighting and bloodshed and which might rightly be called class struggles,—the party strifes raging in Italy and in the world at large constantly interfered with the class struggles and divided the citizens in what one might call a diagonal line, arraying the members of the same class against one another ; and only in some rare cases did party-front and class-front coincide.

This holds good especially with regard to religious discords. Though it happened that a certain class was particularly affected by a religious movement, as when in the beginning of the Reformation in some countries the nobility became protestant, in others the townships, and in some regions the peasant population, such a state of things did not last. Soon all classes in Catholic countries or provinces were fanatic partisans of Rome, whereas in others they stood with equal zeal for the Reformation. It has been shown before that the opinion that the Reformation was but an economic movement in disguise is untenable ; the reasons put forth for it prove insufficient knowledge of facts and rash conclusions.[1] Yet supposing it to be true and demonstrable, that the true causes of the Reformation were of an eco-

[1] Cf. p. 83 *sqq.*

nomic nature, the fact would remain that the poor people, who from class interest ought to have acted quite differently, fought, for the sake of religion, with fanatic zeal by the side of princes and nobles of their creed, against handicraftsmen, workmen and peasants of the opposite persuasion who for similar reasons took the side of their lords. It happened, as we said before, in some cases that the adherents of a religious creed consisted mainly of people belonging to a certain class; the English Puritans, for instance, were chiefly small people, whereas the higher classes were either Catholics or belonged to the Anglican High Church; the Anabaptists in Germany took a democratic and communistic course; a part of the peasants in Salzburg remained Protestant even after the Counter-Reformation. Yet, these were exceptions. In general, members of all classes either took the side of the Roman Church or were against it. If anybody should object that they were not sufficiently enlightened and did not know their class interests, we would reply that this only serves to prove that ideology is decisive, and that neither class interest nor conditions of production are sufficient to produce a certain determined ideology. It proves further that struggles of such world-wide importance as the religious wars for and against the Reformation, which went on for two centuries, were not class struggles and only in a few exceptional cases took the form of, or coincided with, class struggles.

There is further the antagonism and conflict between the generations that plays a very important part in history. It is a conflict which has its roots in economic as well as in ideological elements, and it is being fought out within any class. It has to be admitted that though always and everywhere war is waged between the elder and the younger generation, though their interests are very often opposed to each other, they also have many common interests, interests which are so strong that this war is interrupted by constant truces and that always and everywhere there exist separate federations between the parties. This, however, is the case in many other conflicts. When we consider two nations with conflicting interests, there may be a state of latent and, at times, open war between them. Nevertheless they have a good many common interests, there exist commercial relations and private friendships, and intermarriages between their citizens. To a much larger extent friendly relations of many kinds will be found to exist among members of the different classes. In general, between nations, classes, generations and individuals, it is sometimes the common interests and at others the conflicting interests which turn the scale. At least, it has been so until now. There have always been times when the causes of discord, as conflicting interests, or rather conflicting opinions as to their interests,[1] prevailed and all common interests were forgotten. These were the cases in which a war broke out between nations or a revolution made class struggle acute. For obvious and natural reasons it is the common interests which usually prevail in the struggle between the generations, and an actual outbreak of violence is possible only in individual cases,

[1] Everyone knows that opinions may differ as to what are the interests of an individual, a class or a nation. Errors, false calculations and, above all, misleading influences which may arise from certain individual or class interests, play an important part in determining these opinions. We shall examine this problem more closely in a future work. It is usually neglected and writers are wont to speak of the interests of an individual, of a class or of a nation as if no doubt could exist as to what these interests were.

since for obvious and natural reasons the opposing fronts between them are less sharply defined than between classes and much less than between nations. Yet, in spite of its seemingly peaceful appearance, a ceaseless and often merciless war goes on between two generations, the younger one fighting for the victory of new opinions, new ideas and new institutions, and at the same time craving the positions and the power held by the older one.

The history of mankind is a history of struggles and fighting of every kind. In these struggles the weaker side is beaten, and the path of mankind is marked by oppression and exploitation of the vanquished. It is quite natural that these constant struggles, and the suffering that is their consequence, create a great longing for peace, and that the oppressed and exploited hope for deliverance. Whether these hopes and this longing will ever be fulfilled, and which may be the right path towards fulfilment, is very uncertain. Up to our time, mankind has been similar to the city of which Dante sang :

> Thou shalt behold thyself as woman sick
> Who on her pillow finds no rest at night,
> And seeks to ease her pain by turning quick.

CHAPTER VI

HISTORICAL DIALECTICS

In many writings of Marx and Engels as well as in those of their followers, it is the question of "dialectical development in history". Marx borrowed the term from the philosophy of Hegel. To be sure, in the preface to the second edition of his *Capital* he says that his dialectical method " is the direct opposite to that of Hegel, as Hegel considered reality to be but an appearance of the ' idea ', whereas he considered the ideal to be but the material transformed in man's brains ". In his treatise on *Feuerbach and German classical philosophy*, published in 1888, Engels declared the difference between the two to be the following : according to Hegel the " dialectical development apparent in nature and in history is but a copy, a plaster cast, so to speak, of the eternal self-development of the idea ". Now, he and Marx had done away with this " ideological perversion " ; they considered ideas to be copies and images in man's brain of real things, and not real things to be images of a certain stage of development of the " absolute idea ", exactly as the dialectical conception, according to them, is but a conscious reflection of the " dialectical development in reality ". Thus they thought they had turned Hegel's dialectics upside-down, or rather had put it straight.[1]

All authors, however, agree that Marx borrowed the very idea of dialectics from Hegel, and that, had it not been for Hegel, he would never have thought of a dialectical development of history, though Marx considers the material process and Hegel the ideal as primary.

With Hegel dialectics form a part of logic : every idea contains or produces its own negation, its opposite ; when I entertain the thought " to be " the idea " not to be " follows naturally and at once ; from the thought " I " there follows as naturally the thought " not I " ; from those two thoughts negativing one another results the formation of a new and higher thought in which the contradiction is solved ; yet this new thought gives rise to a new contradiction, which in turn conduces to the birth of a higher thought uniting both. That is the famous " self-development of the idea " according to Hegel. In this manner Hegel succeeded in constructing by pure logical argument not only all philosophy, but all natural science and history as well. At least, he thought he succeeded in doing so. History being, according to Hegel, a continuous self-realisation, a materialisation of the mind, it must necessarily develop and accomplish itself by the same dialectical method.

Marx, on the contrary, considers the real visible developments, the " facts ", as basic ; but seeing the changes and the contradictory tendencies observable

[1] Benedetto Croce in *Materialismo Storico ed Economia Marxista* doubts that the conception of Marx and Engels is really opposed to that of Hegel. He is of opinion that Hegel's conception of history was misunderstood by Marx. Yet even supposing that Engels, in the sentences quoted above, may have used the wrong terms, which is possible, there seems to be no doubt that a difference of this kind exists between Hegel's philosophy of history and that of Marx and Engels.

in different periods, he concludes that the process of historical development is indeed a progression through a series of contradictions. He assumes that whatever exists leads to its own contradiction, any existing state to the contrary state, and these contradictions lead in turn to a higher state of civilisation or form of society, in which the contradictions are dissolved and combined. Such a process, he says, is manifestly a dialectical process. " Marx and Engels ", says Cunow, " espoused Feuerbach's materialistic mode of thought, but they also adopted Hegel's dialectics, removing, however, the dialectical process out of the sphere of ideas and from the self-development of ideas into the material development of society." [1]

Both, Marx as well as Hegel, believe the historical evolution to be dialectical, that is, to proceed through a series of contradictions, which are dissolved in a higher form. The difference between their theories is that Marx believes the " real " historical events to be primary and to be reflected in men's brains and in this way stated by us, whereas Hegel believes that an absolute divine mind is materialising itself in history, the world of events being but its outward appearance and image.

This is at bottom but the old well-known controversy which began in antique times with Plato's doctrine of the ideas, and divided the scholastic philosophers in the age-long contest between Nominalists and Realists by the question whether the abstract or universal notions existed, as the Realists thought, *ante rem*, that is " before the thing " as ideas within the absolute mind or, according to the opinion of the Nominalists, *post rem*, " after the thing ", as mere notions in men's brains. Revived in

---

[1] Cunow, *op. cit.* vol. ii. p. 206.

the seventeenth and eighteenth centuries, the controversy led to the division between Idealism and Materialism.[1] We are not concerned here with this controversy, nor is it our task to examine whether the dialectical method as applied by Hegel in his logic is to be accepted or rejected. His philosophy of history, his conception of history as a whole and as an uninterrupted evolution, gave a powerful impulse to historical science and to thought in general; yet his deductive method of constructing and explaining history led to results which were untenable and even absurd. The dialectics of the Historical Materialists, however, though they may pretend that they are founded on reality, are not a whit better.

There is in all our philosophy, in historical, and to a certain extent even in natural, science a strong residue of scholasticism. Thinkers are still liable to mistake words for the facts denoted by them, to confound the sphere of thought with that of empirical investigation; they frequently believe themselves to be treating of facts while they are only displacing words. Thus Marx and Engels were the dupes of mere words. What they called the " dialectical " development of society is the development from one social system to another which is

[1] At bottom men are the fools of their own incompetence, which they do not wish to acknowledge. Wherever we begin and whatever fact we may accept as basic, no one can deny that it is only in our mind that we become conscious of what we call reality, that we have no other test of this reality but that of our mind, that we are sure only of those " reflections in our brain ", and are unable ever to get beyond them. Everybody, on the other hand, is in a position to state that all mental processes and acts rest upon what are called material processes. We may consider one or the other as primary; start from what basis we like, we are always proceeding in the same vicious circle. The whole controversy is a dispute as to whether the valleys should be considered as hollows between the mountains or the mountains as elevations between the valleys.

considered to be contradictory to it, as, for instance, from Feudalism to Capitalism, from Capitalism to Socialism. They quite lost sight of the fact that terms like " Capitalism ", " Socialism ", " Revolution ", etc., are but sophisticated and artificial expedients to denote a multitude of the most various real facts and processes by one single comprehensive or collective word. They are a kind of spoken stenography. I save the time necessary to tell the reader or the hearer of all the manifold events that happened from 1789 to 1796, by making use of the single expression " French Revolution ", in the expectation that this word will call up in his imagination a vague memory of what he has heard or read about these events, that anyhow he will know what I am talking about. It is, however, no more than a fleeting allusion. The word may perhaps recall to his memory, for a transitory moment, one or the other event ; but it can never and by no means recall the immense variety of facts, the millionfold events of the real French Revolution ; it cannot even give so poor and shadowy an image of it as the ordnance map gives of a landscape. It will moreover call up the most different remembrances and images in different minds. Such words are mere *symbols* ; their comprehensive or collective quality is fictitious, not real.

The word " Feudalism ", for instance, is intended to denote millions of facts, events and institutions which in reality existed in many countries through centuries, which differed widely in the various regions, and yet had a few features in common. The word " Feudalism " is meant, at one time, to call up these common features in the hearer's mind whereas, at another time, it is used with the intention of evoking a vague image of the life of those past times. We cannot dispense with these collective terms, we should be absolutely unable to reason without them, and provided we remain conscious of their being mere symbols denoting a multitude of facts, we may even reach results which are not utterly false. Marx and Engels, however, and their followers, by taking such words as Feudalism, Capitalism, Socialism, for realities, and founding their dialectics upon them, opened a back door to metaphysics, which they believed they had excluded from their system, without being in the least aware of it.

It is perfectly obvious that from any given period we can select the most different kinds of facts and arrange them in some collective term. According to our point of view, or to the object we have in mind, we shall characterise a period by one or the other kind of facts which we have chosen from among the variegated multitude of phenomena which constitute reality. We may, for instance, call the fifteenth and sixteenth centuries, according to the events which are at the moment foremost in our mind and which we therefore select as the most important, the period of religious reform. We may, however, in another mood call this period the age of the incipient struggle between modern absolutism and constitutionalism, or the period of the foundation of the national states, or that of the great geographical discoveries and of a nascent world economy. We may regard the nineteenth century as the time of middle-class domination, as the age of Industrialism or Imperialism or Nationalism, of Liberalism, of Intellectualism, according to the social and intellectual currents and changes which we either personally consider as the most important or which, at this particular moment, we wish to emphasise. This will in turn depend on the point of view from which we consider history in general or that period in particular. The point of view of historians and sociologists, however, changes more or less with successive periods, and even each historian or sociologist will regard different events of a former period as the most important. This is the more inevitable, as not only does the perspective in which we see a former period change of necessity with the lapse of time, but the consequences and results of that period which, if it is not too remote, have since become manifest, or revelations due to further historical research, make us see it in a new light.

We are not only free to choose certain facts or phenomena from among those of a certain period and denote them by some comprehensive term, but it also depends entirely on our point of view which phenomena of another period we shall consider as contradictory to the former, in short, which group or set of facts, opinions and institutions we shall oppose to one another. If, for instance, we comprehend a certain class of political opinions and institutions by the word " Democracy ", we may consider that class of opinions and institutions which we call by a collective word " Aristocracy ", as contradictory to it. We may, however, from another point of view or under the impression of different events consider those aspects which we denote by the word " Dictatorship " as the " negation " of Democracy. We shall certainly prefer to do so at present under the influence of contemporary events, owing to which the main issue at this moment seems to be between Democracy and Dictatorship. We might, however, at another time have regarded " Liberalism " and " Democracy " as opposed to each other. Several authors have certainly done so. Our choice will depend on what particular current in the entire evolution seems at a given time most important to us, and on the course which this current seems to take. What will " of necessity " be the future development of democracy depends solely on the writer's opinion, and his opinion will probably be determined by the fact that certain conflicting currents make themselves particularly felt at the moment. Thinkers generally succumb to the illusion that these currents are permanent phenomena, that the evolution of mankind will proceed in the same direction in which it now seems to tend, and that the same conflicting opinions which agitate the present generation, will upset mankind a thousand years hence. Yet no more than a few decades later, the same currents will present a very different aspect from now, other conflicts will seem important and other contradictory phenomena have come to the fore.

It depends entirely on the point of view which we have chosen, whether we shall find that, in the twelfth and thirteenth centuries, the principal antagonism was that between sensual and joyous worldliness on one hand and religious asceticism on the other, or rather that between the chivalrous culture of the nobles and the new civilisation of the rising cities, or that between a universal monarchy and the sovereignty of the single states. We may even consider the antagonism between the natural economics of the Middle Ages and a beginning return to a monetary system of economics in England and Italy as the most important in the " dialectical " development of the period.

But the whole conception of dialectical development is untenable. It is false that historical evolution invariably proceeds through a series of contradictions. When we compare the principal currents and tendencies in European history since the end of Antiquity — the economic development, the expansion of Christianity and the rise of the Church, the intellectual and artistic development of the race, the continuous struggle between freedom and authority, revolution and reaction — we shall find that the evolution in every single sphere of life proceeds, now by a transition from one state or one tendency to its opposite, and now in an unbroken and straight line ; now at a rapid pace and sometimes very slowly, now gradually and peacefully and at other times through a series of violent conflicts and catastrophes. At times the entire evolution seems to come to a standstill, and conditions remain almost identical for a long period, whereas at other times they change at a feverish speed. The development proceeds, moreover, at a different pace and in varying fashion in different parts of Europe and in the various spheres of life. The different currents of intellectual or social or military or any other development may intertwine, only to separate unexpectedly and take entirely divergent courses at another time. And because it is next to impossible really to understand and to describe this turmoil of events — and even more difficult still to grasp and to unravel the complicated network of causation, the constant and inextricable interworking of natural agencies, of men's brains and of men's hands — the writers, baffled and incompetent, resort to these vague abstractions, these " isms " and " ologies " which are as convenient and indispensable as they are illusive and misleading.

One thing is certain, and it is perhaps the only fact we are sure of in this respect, namely, that this world of man is liable to change, that this change is uninterrupted and is what we call life. It is also indisputable that the change is sometimes slow and gradual and sometimes violent, taking the form of conflict and strife of all sorts. By choosing suitable distances and by selecting those changes and events which seem to be opposed to each other, we shall always be able to state a dialectical contradiction and a dialectical development. The result will be the surer as it is of our own making. It is as if a man should, from the regular series of numbers, select the numbers 1, 4, 9, 16, 25, 36, 49, etc., and then proclaim his discovery that numbers progress by squares. If we select other phenomena less distant from one another, we may find that development proceeds in a straight line. It is the same with the individual. When we consider his life as a whole, we shall find an uninterrupted evolution ; when, however, we compare him as he appears in his sixtieth year with what he was in his twentieth, we shall be sure to find a number of contradictions, at least that between age and youth.

Therefore, what Marx says in *The Poverty of Philosophy*, " No progress without contradiction, that is the law which civilisation has obeyed up to this day ", is a law put forward arbitrarily ; his assertion is undemonstrable and at bottom meaningless, because no one can decide at what moment the new period with its asserted contradiction actually began. History passes on as an uninterrupted ceaseless stream, of which no one knows either the beginning or the end, nor are any man's eyes sharp enough to discover any partition or interruption in its course. The usual divisions into historical periods are artificial and subjective, absolutely extraneous to the events themselves, invented for expediency's sake by one historian and adopted by others, because our intellect, unable to grasp the whole, cannot dispense with divisions and classifications.[1]

The amount of truth in these theories is limited in the first place to the fact that men have different needs and ambitions and are of different opinions on most subjects ; and, secondly, that, for psychological reasons, they are apt to rush from one extreme to the other. These reasons are certainly of a subjective nature ; disappointed, angry and exhausted by the sufferances and difficulties of a certain social state, a system, a government, they are ready to reject all, even what is good and useful in it, and expect salvation from something as new and as different as possible from their present system or state. The new system or state will frequently appear in some sense contradictory to the former. Yet men will do this by no means always nor regularly nor in every respect ; they alter some things and retain others ; many institutions, habits, beliefs remain more or less the same in spite of great social and political changes, while in others only slight deviations are noticeable.

In fact, the development, as we have already pointed

[1] No doubt we adopt objective distinctions for our partition of history into different epochs and periods. It is easy and natural to distinguish between modern and mediaeval history, or between the latter and that of ancient Greece and Rome ; the differences in these cases are marked and real. Yet no one is capable of exactly defining when and where any of these periods has its beginning or its end. We can only state that after a period of dark centuries full of internecine warfare and destruction, there were settled in Europe a group of nations which lived under social conditions and in a state of civilisation very different from those of the earlier days. The beginning of new periods, besides, sets in at different times in different regions : modern history began in reality much later in Russia and in the Balkans than in Central or Western Europe ; one might even say that the beginning of a new period is different in the different strata of one and the same people.

out, is different in the various spheres of life. There may be great changes in the political sphere and very slight changes only in that of domestic life ; economics may change and religious belief remain the same: we find great political and military and some economic changes in France in the last third of the eighteenth century, whereas in England there are at the same time the most momentous economic changes but no political changes to speak of, and in the military sphere none whatever. It may even happen that of two insignificant customs, one falls into desuetude after a short time, whereas the other is preserved through a thousand years. The same may be said of institutions, as well as of systems of all kinds. Changes, always more or less related to a process of creation, and Permanence, mostly akin to imitation, are a thousandfold intertwined in history. Gabriel Tarde has shown that every successful creation is imitated, that waves of imitation emanate from it through time and space, until they either become static and are preserved through a long space of time — many things are done by men to-day just as they were done a thousand years ago — or reach a climax and begin to decline, are pushed aside by other currents of imitation, and disappear.[1] The same fact has been observed and misunderstood by Marx, who, led astray by Hegel, derived from it his untenable theory of dialectics.

To discover or construct a series of contradictions in human history is at bottom only a more or less intelligent pastime and the result no more than a terminology. While believing himself to be in opposition to Hegel and to be basing his theory on reality, Marx was still so much influenced by Hegel as to be unable to see and

[1] Gabriel Tarde, *Les Lois de l'imitation*, 2nd ed. (Paris, 1895).

explain reality otherwise than after the fashion of Hegel. His theory was not the result of a thorough study of history, he did not, as he thought he did, find it by induction, but simply adapted a ready-made Hegelian theory to suit his materialist opinions. All historical materialism is of a deductive and scholastic character. Marx started it, and Engels and others tried to force history into its narrow frame. Marx was unable to free himself from the philosophic training received in his early youth, and his dialectics are no less tainted by scholasticism than those of Hegel.

When a disciple of Marx like Alfred Braunthal comments upon the master's doctrine by saying " whenever the contradictions become too considerable, they can no longer be dissolved by mere progress ", the dialectical phraseology becomes utterly void of meaning. This sentence offers a perfect example of how to render a simple and trivial fact in stilted words for the sake of appearing scientific. Progress in this passage seems to mean a gradual and quiet change undisturbed by acute conflicts. Yet when the contradictions in any given community have become too considerable, a previous peaceful state must already have suffered change. The sentence is but a high-flown paraphrase of the common and natural fact that when party or class dissensions have become violent, a peaceful solution is often impossible. We need no dialectics to know that when men get very angry they often come to blows.

Rather obscure are the words proffered on the subject by Labriola : " Historical dialectics consist only in the recognition of the self-criticism which society applies to itself in the immanent process of its development ".[1]

[1] *Op. cit.* p. 89.

I confess that I am unable to understand what this means, unless the author wishes to state the fact mentioned and described by us on page 162, that a portion of society generally criticises existing conditions and that in this way changes in them are brought about. If this is what is called dialectics, we are agreeable to it, but why then use such a pompous word? In another passage, Labriola, after having explained that " in foreign wars and in domestic conflicts we notice the immense complex of contradictions ", adds that " to Historical Materialism we owe the discovery that contradictions have been the reason and the motive force of all historical events up to our time ". If that is all, we do not owe much to Historical Materialism. For this is only the old truth — in philosophical disguise — that history is a record of many conflicts and that these conflicts produce results.[1]

But the addition that they have been the reason and the motive force of *all* historical events is false. Neither of these sentences conveys any new insight, nor do they seem compatible with Marx's and Engels' original theory of dialectics.

Very different are the utterances of Mr. John Strachey on the subject. He declares with enthusiasm that in " what may be conveniently called the philosophy of Marxism or dialectical materialism, a general pattern has been found to inhere in reality in general. More precisely, this pattern has been found to be characteristic of the movements, or changes, which occur to all types of phenomena. It is a pattern which can be discerned alike in the movement and changes of inorganic and organic matter and in the movements and changes through time of human societies and institutions. Unless we have

[1] Labriola, *op. cit.* pp. 89 and 273.

213

discerned this pattern, it is suggested, we shall find these movements incomprehensible. We shall fail to see any relationship between different classes of phenomena, and our comprehension of their interaction will be limited to mechanical cause and effect. But mechanical movement is only one of a number of ways in which phenomena interact ; there are other, more subtle, but more important, interactions which can be accounted for upon the hypotheses of dialectical materialism alone." [1]

Mr. Strachey has published a very well-written book ; his criticism of the deficiencies of the capitalistic system and his exposition of the theory and practice of socialism belong to the best ever written on the subject. But it is always dangerous when an author ventures dogmatic assertions on subjects with which he is not familiar. Mr. Strachey is certainly neither a historian nor a scientist. Historians will be much surprised to hear that for those among them who do not accept the materialist conception of history, " no such inter-connections between historical events exist ", and that " for them it is just an accident that certain tendencies began to develop at the same time ". Scientists will be no less surprised to learn that "it is dialectics that govern the movements and changes of organic and inorganic matter alike ". This naïve philosophy appears all borrowed from Engels' *Anti-Dühring*. We have shown in a previous chapter how little qualified Engels was for a philosopher. All this is misapprehended Hegelianism. Now what Hegel wrote on subjects of natural science was absurd enough. It was pure mediaeval scholasticism, and it seems a pity that a concoction of it is offered to the workmen of our time as the discovery of an important scientific truth.

[1] *Op. cit.* p. 357.

We can but repeat that dialectics is an arbitrary mode of looking at events and grouping them according to our personal and temporary point of view. It is a pleasurable *jeu d'esprit*, no more.

As a theory it is condemned on its own showing. For according to it, the development through successive contradictions is to go on only until mankind has become communistic. Far from postulating the contradiction to this state, Marx adherents do not even expect it to occur. It is their belief that with the establishment of Communism dialectical evolution comes to an end, as it does for the Jews with the appearance of the Messiah, for the Christians on Judgment Day. These are transcendental events in which men may believe or may not, but which have nothing whatever to do with science or logic. A scientific law that is only to be valid for a certain time and until a certain desirable end is achieved, an end, moreover, the realisation of which, however desirable, has not yet been observed throughout history, is no law at all.[1] Cunow is perfectly right in saying, " Dialectics in connection with Marx's doctrine of historical necessity forms a most important part, a corner-stone of his theory of historical evolution, the elimination of which would involve the collapse of a great part of his theory ". So it is. Both the doctrine of dialectics and that of necessity are equally untenable. They are tombstones, not corner-stones.

Here once more Marx's doctrine offers an instance of an inadmissible combination or rather confusion of science and politics. In order to disguise the fact that

---

[1] An author with whom I do not agree on many subjects, Othmar Spann, has nailed down the same flaw in logic in his book *Der wahre Staat*, 3rd ed. (Jena, 1931).

the demand for a more just and humane distribution of the goods of this earth is a moral demand, that socialism, in short, is a moral end, they declare it to be a logical necessity and their political theory is called " scientific " socialism. Now, theoretical knowledge and practical activity are essentially different and realise themselves on different planes. Science is theoretical, politics practical, activity. A man may found his political activity on scientific experience or make use of scientific knowledge in his political activity ; but scientific experience belongs of necessity to the past and all knowledge is based on past experience ; nobody can base his political theory on future experience which has not yet been made.

Future historical development is hidden from our sight and from our knowledge. We do not know whether a socialist or communist order of society will be introduced in many countries or in all ; and we know still less whether this new society will be durable. That there should ever be a time in which there will be no contradictory opinions, interests and systems, no conflicts between men and no parties, is something which we can hardly imagine, nor do we know whether such a state would be desirable. For the small grain of truth in the doctrine of historical dialectics is that, from the conflict of contradictory opinions and interests and from their discussion, there result new knowledge in the theoretical and new institutions in the practical sphere. The latter are invariably the result of conflicting forces, though this does not imply that they in all cases represent a solution of existing contradictions. That, however, is an age-old experience ; the fact is in striking analogy to a well-known law of physical science, but has nothing whatever to do with dialectics. Whether human nature will change to such a degree that these conflicts will in some future time be decided, as Adolf Goldscheid said, " no longer by the edge of the sword but by the acumen of the intellect ", is unknown to us. It has often been tried and will again be tried whenever circumstances seem favourable, but no one can say whether it will ever be the general rule.

CHAPTER VII

THE DOCTRINE OF NECESSITY ACCORDING TO MARX

THE idea of historical necessity as conceived by Marx and Engels is equally derived from Hegel's philosophy. They admit it themselves and all their followers are agreed about it.

Hegel is of opinion that though all that occurs occurs of necessity, there are nevertheless occurrences which are not necessary, and he assumes that there is a realm of lawless chance. In the same fashion, he assumes that all that is real is reasonable and that nevertheless there exist things which are unreasonable. He finds the solution of this apparent contradiction in the further assumption that whatever is unreasonable is not to be considered as real. Hegel is a scholastic philosopher and like all scholastics he allows himself to be constantly deluded by words. If we believe in necessity, there is no room for chance. Things appear to be the effect of chance from a small human standpoint. Being unable to comprehend the infinite concatenation of cause and effect that takes no heed of his small personal objects and interests, man calls by the name of chance any event which surprises him, because, unaware of the manifold operating causes, he was unable to foresee it. Hegel, however, thought that since in language there existed the substantive " chance " there must needs be a reality corresponding to the word. There is indeed something corresponding to it, but it is the surprise in some person's mind, and not a condition relative to other facts in which the fact stood that caused the surprise. In the same manner things appear reasonable or unreasonable from our human point of view. We call them reasonable or unreasonable according to whether or not they are instrumental towards achieving what we believe to be justifiable or at least intelligible ends.

All this is at bottom playing with words, though there is method in this madness and these word-plays often conceal a meaning that is dangerous to all true knowledge.

That an event occurs is the sole criterion we have of its necessity. All events are necessary which really come to pass. We may reverse this sentence and say : all events that are necessary will really come to pass. If we were able to grasp all existing facts and to understand all the causal connections in the present and in the past—which would require divine intelligence—we would be in a position to explain all past events and to predict the future. Our intellects being much too rudimentary and undeveloped to enable us to overlook and keep in mind more than a very limited number of facts, we cannot even explain the past. As, however, the course of past events appears fixed and immutable, and as a part of them is known to us, we are able in a number of cases to state that some of these events have undoubtedly, or at least with great probability, caused some of the events which followed them. In many cases, however, the causal connection between two successive events is assumed rashly without further proof and investigation. We have given instances of this abuse in previous chapters. As yet, the real occurrence of an event, the existence of a state of things, is the only irrefutable proof of their necessity.

A good many writers are apt to use the term " necessity " in a way which is illogical and inadmissible. Cunow, for instance, explains Hegel's opinions on the subject in the following manner. Circumstances, he says, change, and necessity changes with them ; what is historically necessary to-day may not be so to-morrow ; and as all that is necessary must be regarded as reasonable, what is necessary and reasonable to-day may be unreasonable to - morrow. Thus whatever occurs or exists is apt, by ceasing to be historically necessary, to become unreasonable and absolete.[1] It is obvious that this is equivocating ; the same word is used by Cunow sometimes in one and sometimes in another sense. Necessity, in the philosophical sense of the word, which is also its sense in history, means that something is the inevitable effect of an existing cause and thus is bound to occur. Whatever is not the necessary effect of an existing cause can never be ; what is not necessary in this sense is impossible. Now, Cunow and many writers like him use the word sometimes in this sense and sometimes in that of " appropriate " or of " needed in order to attain a certain end ". It is of course perfectly logical to say : what was expedient yesterday is not so to-day — but that has nothing whatever to do with historical necessity. Unreasonable institutions and senseless actions are as necessary in the philosophical sense of the word as the most excellent ; otherwise they

[1] Cunow, *op. cit.* vol. i. p. 273.

would not exist. Nothing that exists can ever be unnecessary; for its being necessary means that it has
been brought about by a cause, and the most unreasonable and the most injurious actions and measures do not
exist without a cause. But what is or seems expedient
or reasonable can well lose this quality which depends
on changing circumstances and on our judgment which
changes with them.

A few examples will make the equivocation perfectly clear. Discussing the idea of the state in the
seventeenth and eighteenth centuries, Cunow says:
" Economic development in England in the eighteenth
century had the most urgent need of free individuals
with a strong personality who went their way unhampered by superfluous tutelage on the part of the
public authorities and employed their daring and their
efficiency to increase British wealth and British commercial predominance ".

What is the meaning of the " economic development
in England needing such men " ? Do other nations not
need strong personalities ? Yet do they appear whenever they are needed ?

" England needed these strong men " means in
reality that these men appeared and furthered English
wealth and domination. If they had not been born and
had not been able to act, Britain would not have become as rich and predominant in the world. It is that
same " hysteron proteron " which Marx ridiculed in the
German Ideology. " England had a liberal constitution
because it needed strong personalities to develop and
further its commercial predominance " is a teleological
conclusion *ex post*, whereas the truth is that because
England had a free constitution, the strong personalities

had full scope and were in a position to found her commercial empire. That is something quite different and the theoretical inferences that may be drawn from it, are of another kind. If England had been granted a free constitution and strong personalities with the purpose that she might be able to found her empire, there must have been a Providence, a mind to plan this empire and to endow her with a free constitution and strong personalities. This is possible. We are, however, sure that neither Cunow nor the other followers of Marx's theory will accept this. Yet there is no way to evade it : an intention, an object requires a mind to think it ; intentions that nobody ever had, are mere words and nonsense.

It is just as meaningless when Engels writes, " The great monarchies were a historical necessity ". Of course they were ; whatever is or was, without exception, was a historical necessity ; for otherwise it would never have been. But it was no historical necessity in the — unconsciously — teleological sense in which Engels used the word. Cunow comments as follows : " When, in the sixteenth and seventeenth centuries, Capitalism stretched its limbs over Western and Central Europe, the creation of larger unities became a necessity to make further progress possible ".[1]

What is meant by saying that this creation was a " necessity " ? Clearly Cunow does not mean that it was caused by previous events and changes, but that without it a future development would not have been possible. What he meant was that the larger unities were " needed " for this purpose. Using the term in this sense, we shall say : the parcelling out of the large

[1] Cunow, *op. cit.* vol. ii. p. 344.

estates in Eastern Prussia is equally " necessary ", that of the estates in Sicily has long been necessary, yet neither have come to pass. The ruin and expulsion of the peasants in Spain, the yeomen in England, was not " necessary ", and yet it was done. To do away with a great many protective duties is necessary to-day and has been so for years, yet protection continues.

Equally naïve and without sense is what Engels wrote to one of his friends in 1893 : " Napoleon did not come by chance . . . that, if he had not been, another man would have taken his place, is proved by the fact that the man appeared each time when it was necessary — Caesar, Augustus, Cromwell, etc. . . ."

An event or a person is " necessary " in the sense in which Engels and Cunow use the term, from the point of view of a historian, a sociologist, a political man who finds the appearance of a strong man, a saviour, a conqueror, desirable. But from the point of view of historical evolution all is necessary, the creation of large economic unities in the seventeenth century as well as their destruction by the Peace of Versailles.

It is rather astonishing that Engels did not think of the countless cases in which the great man, the hero who was to save the nation, did not appear. None came to save Greece or Rome in ancient times and none to save Spain in 1939. To say that another man would have taken Napoleon's place if he had not been born is as sensible as to say that a man in the next street would have written Shakespeare's plays if he had happened to die in his childhood.

Marx, Engels and Cunow confound necessity and expediency, or fail to see the difference between the two. Accustomed by the philosophical school of the period to look at words and not at facts, they never considered how many different meanings a word may have, how inexact and wavering the usage of language is.

It is much more to the purpose to investigate how it was that when " larger economic unities were needed to make further progress possible ", they were really established ; and how it is that now, though nearly all economists are agreed and have declared and proclaimed at various congresses that the greater part of protective duties ought to be abolished in order to revive trade and redress the world's economy, and that the creation of larger economic unities would be a benefit, it seems nevertheless impossible to bring this about.

Such investigations, however, would show that it is the ideology dominating people's minds at a given time that decides whether appropriate or fatal measures will be taken in an emergency. Problems of all kinds, economic and other, are facing us all the time, and what solution will be found for them depends upon what people think. Their opinions, their insight or their errors are the factors which in the last resort determine what is to be done. And their decision, wise or unreasonable, fatal or felicitous, will always be the one which, under the circumstances, given the mental state of the persons concerned, was necessary and inevitable.

Cunow writes rather carelessly, " National states grew up in Europe, not because it was the sacred right of the nations, but because the historical development took this course ",[1] which is to say, they grew up because they grew up, for their growing-up was the course which historical development took. Words, always words ! In truth it was not because it was their sacred right, but

[1] Cunow, *op. cit.* vol. ii. p. 36.

because the people *believed* in this right, that some nations attained their unity ; in those cases, however, in which the obstacles, the power of those who were opposed to this unity, proved insuperable even to the courage and the energy bred from belief, the nations did not obtain it.

Nearly all the discoveries and interpretations set forth by adherents of the theory are of a similar kind. " The predominance of the middle classes ", says Cunow, " which began in the seventeenth century, was a historical necessity, an inevitable stage of transition through which the evolution of society had to pass." [1] Undoubtedly ! For all dominations which ever existed, were historical necessities, and every stage in the evolution of society was an inevitable one, through which it had to pass in order to reach the next beyond. That follows *ex definitione*. Yet the only proof of this necessity is furnished by the fact that the predominance of the middle class was realised. The historian's task is to investigate why and how this predominance arose at this particular time, and why it was complete and had full sway in some countries and not in others, and why it was realised earlier in some countries and later in others.

The problem is different when the future is in question. History is the science of the past, it is not concerned with the future. Yet, according to the materialist conception of history, the next stage that, of necessity and inevitably, follows on middle-class domination, is socialism. This necessity, however, is not capable of proof. A socialist system has indeed been established in a vast territory, but this was the region in which the " necessary " previous stage of middle-class predomin-

[1] Cunow, *op. cit.* vol. i. p. 87.

ance and capitalism was less developed than in any other part of the civilised world, which was nearer to what Marxists are wont to call the feudal state of society. Socialism realised itself in Russia in direct contradiction to the theory.

There are persons who demand socialism for moral reasons and because they are of opinion that the system is more adequate to the real needs of mankind and to the very exigencies of production by modern technical means. The adherents of Marx, however, refuse to adduce moral reasons. On the contrary, they generally have a dread of ethics akin to that which mediaeval Catholics had of the devil ; their invariable reasoning is that socialism is inevitable and necessary, that it will come according to a " historical law ". They add, however, and Marx himself was of this opinion, that these historical laws are of a different kind and operate differently from the laws of nature.[1] This is perfectly true, for these so-called historical laws are in fact only assertions or assumptions made on the strength of insufficient and uncertain observations. They are, moreover, uncontrollable because history never repeats itself and because experiments under definite and chosen conditions are impossible in history.

If, however, such laws did exist, and if socialism were bound to come according to a law, then it would be quite unnecessary and in a sense impossible to demand what is bound to come to pass of necessity ; if socialism really were the inevitable next stage in the evolution of society, there would be no need of a socialist theory and

[1] Engels, who, as we have repeatedly pointed out, is apt to reason in a very naïve manner, says somewhere that historical laws " appear and disappear". But who is to tell us whether a law that has the habit of appearing and disappearing, is still in force or not ?

still less of a socialist party. Nobody is likely to found a party to bring about spring or summer.

Feeling, however, or we might even say, knowing, though they do not own up to it, that their theory is false, knowing, moreover, from practical experience that very few human actions are automatic, that they are generally brought about by some previous mental or psychic process, they adopt a different method. Being perfectly aware that in order to erect a socialistic system of economy on the basis of certain existing conditions of production, men must first be imbued with a socialistic ideology, they display an indefatigable activity in propagating this ideology, though, if their theory were true, they might spare themselves their pains. Nobody ever made any propaganda for the capitalistic order of society, and yet it came; and nobody knew beforehand that it was necessary and would come.

That a past event was necessary stands to reason; to know this is not to have any special knowledge. To know that a future event which is not of regular occurrence is necessary, is to be a prophet. Now, prophecy and belief may be highly important elements of human life and history, yet they do not belong to the sphere of science. Moreover, the prophecies differ substantially from each other. Marx is of opinion that the state will be abolished in the future order of society, Labriola, Strachey and others are of the same opinion; Cunow and other socialists think differently on the subject.

All that happens and exists is necessary; we need no one to tell us this, or to investigate whether it is true or not. All that is going to happen in the future, will be equally necessary, but we do not know what is going to happen of necessity. We may imagine or believe and predict whatever we like, but we know nothing for certain. What is — partly — known to us is the past, and what remains to investigate is how an event which we deem so important as to call it historical, came to pass and what were its causes. For this is the point at which we may find out what part human agencies, that is, human will and human intellect, had in bringing it about. And — this is very important in order to understand history and politics — if we imagine ourselves at this point, we may say that the past might, *seemingly* and by supposition, have been different from what it *really* and necessarily was. We may say this, putting ourselves in imagination in the place of the people for whom this past was present or future. So much for the past. The future, *our* future, however, may — considering our ignorance of it — be different *in reality* from what *seems* necessary to us. The difference between our knowledge of the past and of the future is the following : we know that all the possibilities which men saw in the past, all the " necessities " in which they believed, were only apparent and imaginary, except the one that realised itself, and so proved to have been the sole real necessity. In the present, however, we are exactly in the same situation as the people of the past were when this past was the present for them ; our imagination shows us a great many future possibilities, and to each person the possibility which he believes to be the one to realise itself, appears as a necessity. Such a belief may, when it is general or when it is shared by many influential persons, cause this possibility to realise itself, unless factors which are still unknown or have not been calculated, stand in its way to prevent it.

When everybody or at least the most powerful class or group in a country are convinced that, in a certain situation, there remains nothing to resort to but war, or that only protective duties can be of avail in a particular economic crisis, then the country will go to war or introduce protection. When they believe the contrary, they will act to the contrary. A particular ideology is, in most cases, the decisive factor in the concatenation of events.[1] And as they know this perfectly well, the socialists are right in making propaganda for their ideas, like all other parties, though, according to their theory, they alone would not stand in need of it.

To quote Cunow once more: "Engels says: Men make their own history. By their actions they pursue certain ends, and these ends as well as the actions, are determined by their opinions of the possibility, the utility, the excellence, the necessity of their object, that is to say, they are determined by their ideology. Their motives, however, their will and their objects are determined by their social state."[2] Engels himself says in his treatise on Feuerbach: "In nature there operate, apart from man, blind unconscious agencies, whereas in the history of mankind the agencies are human persons endowed with consciousness who act either from premeditation or from passion and who pursue certain ends. This does not alter the fact that history is governed by general laws." This is further explained as follows: "Men can rarely do what they intend to do, their many different aims obstruct and thwart one another or prove

---

[1] August Müller, who, it is true, can only conditionally be called a Marxist, says rightly: "Each economic order requires, besides its material pre-requisition, a corresponding economic ideology", *Die Deutsche Volkswirtschaft* (Berlin, 1931), p. 47.

[2] Cunow, *op. cit.* vol. ii. p. 338.

impracticable ; the clashing of all individual volitions and actions creates a state of things in the historical sphere which is perfectly analogous to that of inanimate nature. . . .". [1]

In quoting these two passages, Cunow is obviously unaware that they contain two widely different and even contradictory statements. For the meaning of the second is the following : the actions and volitions of all individuals in a given period neutralise one another so completely that we may as well eliminate and neglect them, for owing to their balancing one another's effect, men's history proceeds exactly in the same way as that of plants, of the earth, of nature in general.

Now it is, in the first place, an arbitrary and perfectly extravagant assertion that all individual volitions and ends neutralise one another completely and that their sum-total is exactly zero. Incidentally, Engels does not even say that this happens in a given period. We have inserted these words. Yet, this sum — zero — which is the result of numberless contradictory forces, all opposing and neutralising each other, must be reached in some definite period of time. Now, what period must elapse in order to realise that effect ? A month, a year, a century, or is the number of opposite actions and volitions exactly the same in every second ? It seems that Engels did not even consider this difficulty — he wrote the sentence without paying any serious attention to it. Moreover, his assertion that the compound action of all that men desire and do, their ideas, passions, reasonable and unreasonable acts, is exactly nil, would have to be proved. A man might as well pretend that

---

[1] Engels, *op. cit.* pp. 43 *et seq.*

all electric forces in the world neutralise each other and are perfectly ineffective.

The fallacy and even absurdity of the whole idea is obvious. For we can clearly see that at all times a number or group of ideas, interests, opinions and desires is preponderant and turns the scales ; otherwise, either no change in our state would be possible or, considering that human thoughts and actions have no influence or effect whatever, the changes would be due to purely chemical and physical processes. This, however, is expressly denied by Engels, who, on the contrary, asserts that the changes are due to those historical and sociological laws whose nature seems to be of an indefinite kind. There are materialist thinkers who hold that all psychic phenomena are at bottom but chemical and physical processes in the cells of the human brain ; but even they do not eliminate human thoughts as necessary links in the chain of causation which in their turn create similar chemical or physical processes in the brains of other men.

But whatever may be the real nature of psychic processes — it is a question which does not concern us in this study — to declare that they balance one another and are ineffectual, and to put in their place mystical laws which are neither of a physical nor of a psychic kind, is so absurd that one is at a loss what to say to such a puerile manner of extricating oneself from a perplexing dilemma. The more so as we all know and see that thoughts and deeds of individuals and of nations take effect after thousands of years. How could cities be built and survive, empires be founded, books be written, the Arctic Regions be discovered, if men's actions and volitions neutralised each other completely ? In order to maintain their theory and make it appear workable, men like Engels and Cunow are ready to clutch at straws and rather to accept the most abstruse impossibilities than to admit what is obvious and what all eyes see and what common sense, unless silenced by a theory, finds out of itself.

When a man submits his accounts to another person and is reproached with certain items being wrong, he cannot excuse himself by saying that the mistakes in his account balance each other and that the sum is right nevertheless ; but he is bound to prove this by a minute examination of every item of his addition. The assumption that a sum composed of countless uncontrollable items is in each case exactly zero is fantastic to a degree, which makes it impossible to discuss it seriously.

Furthermore, we are told in the same breath that all men's thoughts and the motives of all their actions are determined by the social conditions. If this be the case, there is no need of this curious arithmetical hypothesis. It is certainly more rational to assume that men's various activities determined by social conditions are necessarily leading to certain predetermined social and historical changes than to accept the supposition that they have no result at all and that the changes are brought about without any contribution on their part by those strange demi-gods called laws. At bottom both arguments are equally gratuitous ; for it has been shown that the social conditions are not the sole real causes.

In treating the questions of determinacy and necessity, the adherents of the materialist conception of history are constantly resorting to tautologies without being aware of it. " Marx and Engels ", says Cunow, " do not explain the necessity of socialism by the fact that it is a prerequisite for attaining men's highest aims or that it is far superior to capitalism . . . no, Marx explains the necessity of socialism by the fact that it is an inevitable consequence of the tendencies inherent in capitalistic society and its sole possible successor." [1] What is the difference between being necessary and being inevitable ? We are not much enlightened by being told that socialism is necessary because it is inevitable. Those who pronounce such sentences are the first victims of the deception contained in them. This has been pointed out before. The sole criterion of the necessity of an historical event being that it has realised itself, Cunow in order to express himself correctly, ought to have said : " Marx and Engels prophesy the coming of socialism from the tendencies inherent to capitalism and they believe that it is an inevitable consequence of these tendencies ". Like other prophecies, this one may come true or not. It is a question which is beyond the sphere of history and of science in general.

The same may be said of the question whether the introduction of a socialist system would be desirable and beneficial or not. This question is of a political nature and is not the subject of our study. What is said in it does not prove anything either for or against socialism. We are exclusively concerned with the historical theory of Marxism.

From what has been said in this and in the previous chapters, the following results emerge so far as this theory is concerned :

In the first place, the productive forces do not play the part in history that Marx and his followers ascribe to them.

[1] Cunow, *op. cit.* vol. ii. pp. 337-8.

Secondly, it cannot be proved that all legal, political, religious and other intellectual phenomena, all that Marx and his adherents call the " ideological superstructure ", are determined by the conditions of production. Yet, though it is impossible to prove this, it is in many cases easy enough to prove the contrary.

We are entitled to assume, and it can in many cases be proved, that the conditions of production have an important influence on the laws and on the different activities, customs and opinions of men, much more important than was thought in former times ; neither has this influence been given due consideration in former historical works. The inter-connection of cause and effect in these complicated social phenomena, however, is difficult to trace and generally uncertain ; it cannot be doubted that many other factors co-operate in bringing about the results and alter them ; neither can it be doubted that a great many individual and social phenomena develop independently of the conditions of production. The conditions of production are, moreover, themselves dependent on, and determined by, various other phenomena, particularly of an intellectual nature, whereas the productive forces, though belonging to these phenomena, do not play an active part in creating the conditions of production.

In Marx's theory, a number of phenomena are segregated from the infinite connection of events and declared to be basic ; according to other theories other phenomena are treated in this way ; no one, however, has yet been able to furnish the necessary proofs.

The same may be said of class struggle. From among the countless struggles and conflicts filling the annals of history, the authors of the theory selected class struggles for the reason that from their point of view they seemed particularly important, and they declared them to be the only decisive factor.

Marx's description of the great social revolutions and his classification of historical periods has been shown to be erroneous, and it has been demonstrated that his dialectics and doctrines of historical necessity are vague, founded on a delusion produced by mere words and on a false idea of real historical developments.

In no way and in no part is the theory sufficient to explain historical events and their causation.

CHAPTER VIII

THE PART PLAYED IN HISTORY BY ECONOMICS

In the preceding chapters we have set forth the fallacies and the numerous errors in the Materialist Conception of History, and we believe we have demonstrated how utterly inadequate it is to explain historical evolution and the causal inter-connection of events.

Completely to explain the causal concatenation in history so as to set the question at rest is impossible. For, aside from the fact that scientific research did not seriously begin until a few generations ago and that every decade lays bare new worlds of the past, it is evident that our intellect, being unable to overlook and understand more than an insignificant number of facts and elements, is in no way equal to the task of really understanding the world and its history. It must be a curiously self-satisfied and shallow mind that imagines itself able to grasp what is impossible of cognisance, at least in our present state of development.

Faced by an infinity of phenomena of which we have ourselves witnessed only a very small part, while others have been transmitted to us, in a more or less truthful and reliable form, by records from the past, we endeavour to find or to construct a certain logical order, a causal connection in the mass of events, witnessed or

236

handed down. These endeavours are only partially successful.

In this chapter we shall try to show in broad outlines the true relations between the economic and other phenomena in historical evolution as they appear to the mind unbiassed and unblinded by a preconceived theory. A closer investigation of these relations must be deferred.

In view of the fact that man's very existence depends upon his economic activity, it is surprising that the study of economics has not engaged the attention of historians and philosophers from the earliest dawn of recorded history. It is, however, noticeable that men carefully record all that is unusual, and do not consider matters of daily occurrence worthy of their attention. It is for this reason that wars, earthquakes, crimes and epidemics, the lives of notorious individuals, were chronicled long before men gave anything but practical attention to the daily life of the community.[1]

It was the extraordinary economic development in modern times as well as the great financial needs of the modern state which caused men to realise the importance of private economics to public finance and, consequently the significance of economics in politics, law and civilisation in general. It is, however, another of man's habits to rush from one extreme to another and to try to correct one blunder by making a worse. Thus, having for so long neglected the study of economics, man began to overestimate its importance, and there soon appeared a school of philosophers and scientists who maintained that economic conditions were the ultimate causal factor

[1] Alfred Marshall, in the Introduction to his *Principles of Economics* (London, 1891), gives other reasons for this neglect which, no doubt, are true also, but which, I think, were secondary.

which determined all important trends in history. That is the theory which we have discussed and subjected to examination in this study.

The question is : In what way did man's economic activity influence and determine his development ? We know that man produced commodities or goods in order to satisfy his needs. This is as true of a troop of savages in the diluvian period as of the capitalistic society of the United States. Men's needs increase with the growth of civilisation, production expands with them and proceeds by ever more complicated methods.

Although no record from these remote times has reached us we may be certain that man from the beginning had to compete with wild beasts and with hostile human beings for food and shelter. In this struggle, primitive man, without natural arms and clothing, lacking the strength and speed of many of his competitors and the fecundity of others, was severely handicapped and, for this reason, was only able to exist by combining together in troops and tribes. Even thus he would have proved no match for the formidable predatory beasts of that period, had he not been able to avail himself of his intellectual endowments and consequent power of combination and invention. It was by his mental abilities that he was able to survive his dangerous enemies, and by this same quality he was enabled to develop economically.

In order to follow this development, it is necessary to realise that only a few of man's needs are of a primary nature : his need of food and shelter and his sexual appetites. So far, man is in much the same situation as the animals. All further needs are created by his intellect. Some one man must have been the first to fix a sharp stone or a pointed bone to a stick. It was a new idea, and immediately all the other members of his tribe felt the need of the same sort of weapon.[1] Again, when one man began to decorate himself with shells or plumes, others felt the need for similar adornment. All the numberless needs of mankind spring from ideas and spread by imitation. By commerce whole nations learnt fresh needs from other nations. It is the same in our own time. We learn to feel the same wants as others, we want what they have. As a rule, the means to satisfy the need is there before the desire itself, and man feels the need because he sees or hears of the means to satisfy it. Invention, that is intellectual activity, creates the commodity, and imitation, likewise an intellectual process, creates demand. When man realised that animals could be domesticated, that he could break in a horse by sitting on it, pressing its flanks between his legs and putting a cord in its mouth, that mares and cows could be milked, and calves and lambs bred and fed, he evolved from a mere hunter into a cattle-breeder and a nomad. When he learnt to put seed into the earth and gather the fruits thereof when it had grown, he became a peasant. When he acquired the knowledge of the use of the wedge in the form of knife, axe and saw, and learnt how to use various kinds of wood and stone, straw and reeds, clay and lime, he could build himself a house. Every change in the methods of production and all advance in the manufacture of the commodities necessary to satisfy his growing needs was achieved by intellectual activity and was ultimately due to man's

[1] No doubt there were many inventors of these simple instruments in different parts of the world. This does not alter the fact that wherever it happened it was an intellectual achievement.

intellectual development. A savage hunter who, several thousand years ago, discovered a deadly poison for his arrows, and an engineer who to-day constructs a self-acting brake, have both set their minds to work and bestowed thought upon the matter. It is therefore clear that changes in methods of production can take place only by means of brainwork, discovery and invention.

It has been asserted that it was by his economic wants that man's intellect was developed. This may be true in the sense that practical problems gave his intellect occasion to develop ; but it is false if meant to imply that wants are to be regarded as the cause and intellect as the effect. If this were true, the animals would but have to feel needs in order to develop human intelligence ; whereas it is perfectly clear that they do not feel any needs beyond those primary requirements mentioned above, because they lack the necessary intelligence. We may, therefore, conclude that intellectual development depends partly on agencies as yet unexplained, such as race and individual heredity, and such additional causes as a favourable situation or the proximity and example of a more advanced race. We are drawn to this conclusion because we find, on the one hand, in the same regions, one race in an advanced state of civilisation and another primitive, while, on the other hand, we find branches of the same race, one civilised and the other savage. It may well be that progress was due to the " chance " of heredity, to the union of a particularly well-matched couple which procreated the intelligent and enterprising individual who took the lead.[1] The

[1] Toynbee is of opinion that the oldest Egyptian and Sumerian civilisation arose because climatic changes, which made existence impossible in

highest civilisation in South America was found in the highlands of Peru. Now, either the Indians of Peru must have been a particularly gifted branch of the red race, or there were particularly gifted individuals born among them, or, as Gobineau thinks, men of a foreign race came to their country whose civilisation they made their own by imitation.

Primitive man did not like work; he liked it even less than civilised man does now. All our knowledge of savage tribes, as well as the records we have from ancient times, prove that, above all, primitive man is lazy. He may love to hunt or to fight, because these exertions are exciting enjoyments and satisfy his pride in his own strength; but he does not love regular work, which he leaves to women and slaves. Even modern man is not over-fond of it and likes to avoid it. It was dire necessity, or coercion, which implies necessity, that induced him to work. The strong and powerful men of the tribe shunned it and forced their womenfolk or men whom they had captured, to work for them.

We may take it for granted that even in primitive times, when men had few and simple needs, the head

those regions in which they had lived until then, caused some primitive tribes to drain the swampy deltas of the Nile and of the Euphrates, whereas other tribes, who were incapable of a similar " dynamic reaction ", either perished or migrated to other regions where they continued their former primitive mode of existence.

This seems at bottom exactly the same thing, for it was, in the first place, the energy and the mental qualities of those tribes, and most probably the intelligence and efficiency of some individual members, that conduced to the progress described. Cf. Arnold J. Toynbee, *A Study of History*, vol. i. (2nd ed., Oxford and London, 1935), p. 302.

Childe, in his work *The Most Ancient East*, quoted by Toynbee, seems to hold that, owing to similar climatic catastrophes, primitive man learnt to become a cattle-breeder and an agriculturist. One would indeed think that the draining of the swamps and the necessary cutting of canals pre-supposes a considerable degree of civilisation.

of the family or the strongest man of the tribe, who was its chieftain, in most cases took for himself the best part of the booty or whatever the tribe's acquisitions were. It is further probable that at a very early period the difference of sex and age led to a natural division of labour, the women and the young being charged with certain works or services. When some tribes had become cultivators or when they led a wandering life as nomads, a further division of labour grew up, due to the fact that some persons had a special aptitude for making tools or arms or for managing horses, and so on.[1] And though fields and pastures might be in common, the chiefs and those who knew how to appease the dreaded spirits, the conjurors and priests, had their privileges, which generally consisted in the possession of more goods and more women. But by far the most important cause of inequality, a cause which at the same time meant a certain organisation, became effective when men ceased to eat their prisoners but kept them, or some of them, as slaves, in order to work for their masters.[2]

The dangers which threatened the existence of the savage and half-savage tribes, gave an extraordinary authority to the strong man, the great hunter and

[1] Cf. Herbert Spencer, *Principles of Sociology* (London, 1896), vol. iii. pp. 334 *et seq.*

[2] In the *German Ideology* it is said that the division of labour only began to be real and effective when it became a division into intellectual and manual work. This is obviously false. The division into free men who fought and enjoyed life, and slaves who did the household and agricultural work, was certainly effective enough. We may agree as to what is said on the next page, that the division of labour implies an unequal division of the produce ; this, however, is not a consequence of the division of labour itself, but, like this very division, is due to the overriding power of the masters. In all these utterances Marx and Engels prove themselves to be mere theorists, heedless of reality and practice. Cf. *Deutsche Ideologie*, pp. 21, 22.

fighter who protected and at the same time dominated the other tribesmen. The need of protection, gratitude and fear, on the one hand, lust of power, the elated feelings and the real advantages which power bestowed, on the other, combined to strengthen such ascendancy. Religious feelings, often deliberately invoked and fomented by the powerful, consolidated it. With the extension of territory owing to conquest or to the union of several tribes under the same rule more complicated organisation became necessary. A gradation of power, a kind of hierarchy, was introduced, with the result that the difference between those who commanded and those who obeyed became more accentuated.

In savage times robbery is natural. A stronger tribe drove a weaker one from the hunting-grounds; a wandering troop of warriors raided a village of peaceful peasants, killed the men and carried off the women and the cattle. To plunder even in times not distant was the simplest and most natural way of enriching oneself. The nomadic tribes of hunters and cattle-breeders had as a rule more warlike propensities than the sedentary agricultural peoples. Hunting and pastoral tribes have always been raiders and formidable warriors. For an agricultural people it means much to abandon their homesteads, to change all their habits, and to wander into unknown lands towards an uncertain destiny. Only necessity or a great hope can make them take such a resolution. A long series of bad harvests, oppression by powerful neighbours, internal discord, may be the reason — not over-population, which scarcely existed in those times — and perhaps sometimes the attraction that rich fruitful countries had for people who cultivated barren soil under an inclement sky. It is natural for hunters and nomads to wander, and to fight when encountering a hostile tribe. Whenever a prospect of better pastures or of rich spoil allures them, they are quickly resolved ; even the mere lust of adventure suffices. Whenever they became united in a somewhat bigger body, or if a federation of tribes was formed, they would not hesitate to set out on conquest. They sought plunder and pleasure, but their object was not to gain an " unearned income " ; it was not economic in this sense. They might carry off young women, jewels and gold and perhaps slaves, but what they most desired was to fight and to destroy, to kill the men, to burn the towns and villages and to let their horses trample down the fields. It took a long time before they considered themselves as the proprietors of the conquered lands and learnt to spare the people and to live on the produce of their subjects' work.[1] In order to do so, they had to settle down, and they did not like that. The cases, however, in which they did were important in history.

Thus the nomadic and semi-nomadic horsemen of Iran subjugated the Near East and made the populations of the conquered regions tributary ; in the same way, though driven by the strong impulse of a religious idea, the Arabs conquered a great part of Asia, northern Africa and Spain ; the Seldjuks, the Osmanli, the Mongol hordes overrode whole continents, destroying civilisation and founding new empires. The Germans,

---

[1] " This first step toward civilisation takes a long time, for primitive man is essentially a fighter ; he does not want to own things, he wants to destroy them. He enjoys proving his strength in doing so, and he only feels his own power completely by annihilating human beings and lifeless things ; just as our children enjoy breaking their toys ", G. d'Avenel, *Histoire économique de la propriété, etc.* (Paris, 1910), vol. v. p. 68.

when they invaded the Roman Empire, were semi-nomads ; they were hunters and cattle-breeders rather than peasants, and, above all, they were warriors. All these nations, as well as later conquerors, became the ruling class in the conquered countries. They were a class of the great landed proprietors, while the native population cultivated the soil for them. They levied taxes on the towns, the merchants and the people, but they took upon themselves the defence of the country and of its unwarlike inhabitants.

Although, owing to the fact that men are of unequal strength and abilities, an aristocracy made its appearance everywhere " as cream rises in the milk ", yet in the great majority of cases a conquering foreign race formed the nobility of the land, while the indigenous nobles either were destroyed or sank to a lower social level, or, at least in part, merged with the new rulers. This happened in India, in the Persian Empire, in many of the Greek and Macedonian states and in the Roman Empire. The Germans became the ruling class in the feudal kingdoms which arose from the ruins of this Empire,[1] and so did the Normans in England, the English in Ireland, the Germans in the Slav and Baltic countries, the Turks in the Balkans, the Spaniards in South America. As a rule, though not always, the two races coalesced, in course of time, into one nation with a common language. This, however, does not alter the

[1] When the Lombards conquered and occupied a large part of Italy, they killed the Roman nobles and appropriated their estates. The lesser Romans became " Lites ", that is, half-free men. Yet even within the same race warlike ability was decisive to such a degree that those of the conquering Germans who, having settled down on Roman ground, became peaceful peasants, soon lost their caste and were made serfs. Cf. Hans Delbrück, *Geschichte der Kriegskunst*, vol. iii., " Das Mittelalter ", pp. 33 and 44.

fact that the nobility and the common people were originally of different race.

It was superior bodily strength and valour, and often superior intelligence, which caused the inequality of wealth and possessions; it was Power which determined the economic as well as the political constitution of a people, and not the reverse.

It was because Marx and Engels devoted their attention exclusively to the vicissitudes and the development of the conditions of production within the different societies that they entirely overlooked the relations of an international kind between these societies. The latter factor has been at least as important, but was treated by them only incidentally and without any real interest.[1]

Economic production itself gives no power. If this had been the case the workmen would have been the nobles, whereas, in fact, the working population has never anywhere been much esteemed, and to work, especially in former times, was considered low-born and degrading.[2] It was the strong man, the warrior, who was held in high esteem, and beside him, owing to his power to intercede with the gods, the priest, whose authority was sometimes even greater. In many countries, as, for instance, in Greece and Rome, priests and nobles formed one class.

The possessions which were assigned to the great, or which they appropriated by main force, of course increased their power. They could use them to make friends, to hire servants and soldiers, buy arms, and fortify their castles. For this reason, kings, princes and

---

[1] I know perfectly well that Engels was very much interested in, and conversant with, international relations in the nineteenth century, but that has nothing whatever to do with the part he ascribes to them in his theory.

[2] Cf. p. 53.

nobles always strove after money and riches, which they did not produce.[1] Yet, though wealth heightened their power, it was power that brought wealth, and not the reverse. Not economic qualities and achievements, but warlike qualities and deeds were decisive. If persons who lacked power acquired riches by peaceful means, they did not retain them long.[2]

Rich merchants like the Phoenicians and Carthaginians and, in later times, the merchants of Florence, Venice, Genoa and the Hanseatic League, were either themselves warriors or hired warriors to fight for them.

It was not until peaceful producers and merchants were effectively protected by the law that they could enjoy their riches in security. This was demonstrated during the long peaceful period of the Empire of the Romans. A similar state of security did not recur in Europe until the seventeenth century. Yet the Roman knights, who were the capitalists of the time, generally

---

[1] For the protection which the powerful warriors gave to the lowly producer, they might justly demand to be paid in taxes and duties. They also administered justice and governed the land, and we are far from underrating such services, which, though often badly done and insufficient, were necessary for maintaining order and making production possible. It is true that by their constant warfare they often destroyed more than they saved by their protection.

[2] To mediaeval man this was perfectly clear. A law of King Ervig of the Visigoths that was issued in the year 681, vituperates those who "maiorem diligentiam rei familiaris quam experientiam habent in armis, quasi laborata fruituri possideant, si victores esse desistunt". These words came true twenty years later; in one single battle the Arabs made an end to the reign of the Visigoths, who had lost their martial vigour.

"The strong man was more than the rich man until the seventeenth century," says d'Avenel; "before this time money alone was of little use". Cf. G. d'Avenel, *Études d'histoire sociale. La Noblesse française sous Richelieu* (Paris, 1901), p. 289. "During the Middle Ages people grew rich, not by production, but by violent change of ownership. . . ." "The only way to get rich, the only possible speculation was to fight." Cf. G. d'Avenel, *Histoire économique de la propriété, etc.*, vol. v. pp. 4, 43.

served in the army; and the ennobled lawyers and bankers in France and Italy let their sons become officers, because a military rank conferred a much higher position in society than all their wealth.

Virtuous economists of the nineteenth century believed that capital had its origin in the savings of industrious workmen and merchants. It is true that capital itself, the goods of which it consists, were created by work. They owe their existence to the intelligence of the gifted men — physicists, inventors, engineers — who found the methods to produce them, and to the interminable work of millions of hands. But the possession of these goods in such quantity as to form riches was rarely due to work and industry. From the earliest times to this day the skilful and painstaking workman might earn a moderate income, but could grow rich only in quite exceptional cases. Better were the chances of the merchant, provided that he carried on his trade on a large enough scale and knew how to protect himself. But from the first invasion of peaceful countries by warlike nomads to the foundation of the feudal states and the exploitation of modern colonies, great riches were acquired by main force and by constraining the producers to yield a considerable part of their produce to a small class of lords or rajahs or planters, or whatever they might call themselves.

Karl Marx himself shows in the twenty-fourth chapter of his *Capital* that modern capitalism was chiefly created by force and violence. It derived its origin from a fourfold source; in the first place, the seizure of church lands; secondly, the expropriations of the peasants in Italy, Spain, England and other countries in the fifteenth and sixteenth centuries; thirdly, the importation of large quantities of gold from the New World, gained by oppression and exploitation of the natives ; and, finally, the great government loans which brought immense gains to the bankers at a time when law and order had become such that these gains were safe and remained in the hands of those who had made them.[1]

This proves that neither the " productive forces " nor the " conditions of production " are the primary causal factors in history. Marx tries to delude himself and his readers by declaring that " force is an economic agency " ; but this is mere sophistry. By thus playing on words, you can prove anything. Gobineau, who believes that race is the factor which determines everything in history, might in the same manner call production or climate " racial " agencies. Marx is equivocating by using the word " economic " in a double sense. An economic agency is an agency of an economic nature, whereas Marx in this place employs the word in the sense of an agency influencing or determining economics. Using the word in this sense, there is nothing that might not be called an economic agency.[2] War, epidemics, the sun would all be economic agencies ; intellect, politics, religion, laws would no longer be parts of the superstructure ; they would become economic agencies. This one utterance of Marx suffices to show the hollowness and sophistry of the entire theory.

Force, in olden times, was not an economic agency, but the agency that determined economics. In modern

[1] Cf. Karl Marx, *Capital*, vol. i. ch. 24 ; and W. J. Ashley, *An Introduction to English Economic History and Theory* (2nd ed., London, 1893), vol. ii. ch. iv.

[2] Engels is guilty of the same equivocation when he speaks somewhere of " race, an economic potency ".

times, however, it ceased to be decisive. Security became such that, at least within the territory of civilised countries, one could no longer grow rich by employing force. At the same time commerce and industry, owing to the new means of transport, gained an importance such as they had never had before. Now indeed the possession of great wealth meant power, such power that the military and hereditary classes, which before had wielded all authority and laid down the law, had to give way before it. The situation became such that, whereas in former times riches had been subject to power, power had now, as a rule, to further the interests of the rich.

However, we must not let ourselves be deceived by all these misleading abstract and collective expressions like " power ", " capital ", etc. History and Political Economy are being written as if objects like goods, capital, institutions could develop spontaneously and without man's participation. People write and talk as if the goods and the institutions mentioned in historical and economic treatises could develop of themselves, whereas in reality none of them can come into existence or change without its form or the supervening changes having first been thought and planned by the human mind and carried into effect by human will. Capital — riches, wealth or by whatsoever name you may call it — has no power. It is something dead, a soulless thing, deprived of all will of its own. But a *man* who owns capital may have power. All the momentum is in his mind, in the impulses, thoughts and ideas which determine his will. Everybody, of course, knows this ; he knows that by saying " Capital has power ", or " Democracy is on the decline ", or " Prices are rising ", he means " The capitalists have power ", " The democrats are losing influence or energy and their number is decreasing ", " Men sell or buy their goods at higher prices " ; and yet, by constantly using these expressions, people are liable to forget the real nature of things.

When we say that in former times wealth was subject to power, whereas at present power is subject to wealth, what we really mean to say is that formerly a man had to have power — bodily strength, authority, or warriors at his service — if he desired to gain riches and to keep them, whereas to-day, as a rule, a man has to be rich in order to have power. In the eleventh century some five hundred Norman knights could make themselves masters of southern Italy, while those who were rich without being brave and powerful, had to serve them and yield part of their wealth to them. On the other hand, the Florentine bankers of the thirteenth century, though they could substantially further the policy of the Popes and of the French kings by lending them money, could not think of imposing a certain line of conduct upon them. Nowadays, men who are very rich, though they may be neither strong nor brave nor respected, are in a position to determine the policy of a government and may force it to make war or keep the peace.

But the richest state must even to-day spend a large part of its wealth on means of power, on soldiers and ships, otherwise it would soon be deprived of its riches, for the simple reason that international relations are still regulated chiefly by force. If England had no formidable fleet, her colonies would soon be lost, the Empire would crumble, her power would end. Her wealth is but an instrument : it is the nation's will to maintain England's power that determines her armaments.

It would, however, be a gross mistake to believe that

the present state of things, the fact that law secures a man's possessions and thus makes possible the power of capitalists, is due to economic causes. Modern government and administration as well as economic developments in modern times were both created by human intellect ; both are due to the progress of science, to the " eternal spirit of the chainless mind ". Railways, gas, electric light and the telegraph made a more effective police and a better administration of justice possible. The discoveries of scientists created the modern state and made modern capitalism possible. The conditions of production did not " change ". These intransitive forms of verbs are equally misleading. People will also say : " costume has changed since the last century " ; but neither costume nor production are capable of changing by their own impulse ; both are changed by men, and man will change production as soon as he is shown a better and more efficient method.

The intellectual movement in Europe, the fight for intellectual freedom, began in the thirteenth century. It was soon crushed and silenced in the Islamic countries, but in Europe it continued. It revived in the fifteenth and sixteenth centuries and was called the Renaissance and Humanism ; at this time it was favoured by nearly all the courts of Europe and by a great part of the aristocracy, that is to say, by the existing organisations of power. The new intellectual freedom made possible modern science and philosophy, which involved a critical investigation of the nature of things. Then began an era of scientific discoveries and technical progress. The movement spread in a thousand ways, by influences which operated daily and hourly, in many thousand places ; by books, by lectures, by many thousand discussions and conversations in private rooms, by new laws, by reforms and revolutions. Thus, by constant operation in the complicated machinery of life it changed the political as well as the economic state of mankind. Those, however, who held the power, and who in the beginning had favoured the movement, soon began to find it dangerous, and employed the technical means which it had created, in sundry attempts to arrest and to crush it. We need not enter into the details of this contest, which goes on to this day.

It was human intellect which from the beginning invented the instruments and determined the methods of production. It was, however, not allowed freely to decide, because the powerful and strong, from the beginning to this day, intervened and enforced a distribution for their own benefit of the work and of its product. Their power was at first based upon bodily strength, but they soon employed intellectual means also, though they always appeal to physical means in the last resort. When we bear in mind that the terms Production, Intellect, Power denote groups of phenomena whose limits are not always to be defined by a clear-cut line, though everyone knows more or less what is meant by them, we may sum up in the following way : Production is due to need ; the methods of production depend solely on the degree of intellectual development attained by mankind ; Power and Intellect combine to determine who is to do the work as well as the distribution of the product. Intellect and Power appear to be the two causal factors which, all through history, determined the economic and political state of mankind.[1]

[1] We have repeatedly had occasion to remark that the terms " mode of production " and " conditions of production " are vague, that the pheno-

We have now stated the real causal relation between those groups of phenomena which are denoted by the terms " power ", " economics ", " intellect " — no more. This relation is very different from that which is adopted in the materialist conception of history. Yet in order to understand historical events and developments, it is necessary also to arrange and consider them from points of view quite other than those chosen up to now. That, however, would be a task beyond the limits of this critical study.[1]

mena denoted by them are in part identical, and that the authors who make most use of them, by no means always have a clear understanding of what is meant by them. Not even what is meant by production is incontrovertibly established ; at any rate, authors are not agreed on the question as to what activities are to be considered as being productive. Yet though the limits of the term may be contested, its general meaning is undoubtedly the production of goods.

It is much more difficult to distinguish between the mode and the conditions of production, two terms which are used indiscriminately by Marxist authors. It seems advisable to call " mode of production " the form and the methods of the activities by which a community of men produce goods for the satisfaction of their needs, whereas we understand by " conditions of production " the relation in which the members of the community participate in producing those goods as well as in disposing of the goods produced, and the methods of distribution. Considering production from a technical and economic standpoint, we shall find the mode of production, whereas by studying it from a social standpoint, we shall be informed of the conditions of production. At least in this study these terms are to be understood in the way described.

[1] The author of the present study is preparing a work under the title *Essay towards a Phenomenology of History*, in which the nature of historical necessity, the part played by Power, by Intellect and by Economics, the rôle of the individual and that of the masses, will be more closely examined, and the real inter-connections and causal links in history, as far as they are accessible to the human mind, will be shown.

APPENDIX I

MARX'S FIFTEEN PROPOSITIONS IN THE ORIGINAL

I. In der gesellschaftlichen Produktion ihres Lebens gehen die Menschen bestimmte, notwendige, von ihrem Willen unabhängige Verhältnisse ein, Produktionsverhältnisse, die einer bestimmten Entwicklungsstufe ihrer materiellen Produktivkräfte entsprechen.

II. Die Gesamtheit dieser Produktionsverhältnisse bildet die ökonomische Struktur der Gesellschaft, die reale Basis, worauf sich ein juristischer und politischer Ueberbau erhebt, und welcher bestimmte gesellschaftliche Bewusstseinsformen entsprechen.

III. Die Produktionsweise des materiellen Lebens bedingt den sozialen, politischen und geistigen Lebensprozess überhaupt.

IV. Es ist nicht das Bewusstsein der Menschen, das ihr Sein, sondern umgekehrt ihr gesellschaftliches Sein, das ihr Bewusstsein bestimmt.

V. Auf einer gewissen Stufe ihrer Entwicklung geraten die materiellen Produktivkräfte der Gesellschaft in Widerspruch mit den vorhandenen Produktionsverhältnissen oder, was nur ein juristischer Ausdruck dafür ist, mit den Eigentumsverhältnissen, innerhalb deren sie sich bisher bewegt hatten.

VI. Aus Entwicklungsformen der Produktivkräfte schlagen diese Verhältnisse in Fesseln derselben um.

VII. Es tritt dann eine Epoche sozialer Revolution ein.

VIII. Mit der Veränderung der ökonomischen Grundlage wälzt sich der ganze ungeheure Ueberbau langsamer oder rascher um.

255

IX. In der Betrachtung solcher Umwälzungen muss man stets unterscheiden zwischen der materiellen und naturwissenschaftlich treu zu konstatierenden Umwälzung in den ökonomischen Produktionsbedingungen und den juristischen, politischen, religiösen, künstlerischen oder philosophischen, kurz ideologischen Formen, worin sich die Menschen dieses Konflikts bewusst werden und ihn ausfechten.

X. So wenig man das, was ein Individuum ist, nach dem beurteilt, was es sich selbst dünkt, ebensowenig kann man eine solche Umwälzungsepoche aus ihrem Bewusstsein beurteilen, sondern muss vielmehr dies Bewusstsein aus den Widersprüchen des materiellen Lebens, aus dem Konflikt zwischen gesellschaftlichen Produktivkräften und Produktionsverhältnissen erklären.

XI. Eine Gesellschaftsform geht nie unter, bevor alle Produktivkräfte entwickelt sind, für die sie weit genug ist, und neue, höhere Produktionsverhältnisse treten nie an die Stelle, bevor die materiellen Existenzbedingungen derselben im Schosse der alten Gesellschaft selbst ausgebrütet worden sind.

XII. Daher stellt sich die Menschheit immer nur Aufgaben, die sie lösen kann, denn genauer betrachtet, wird sich stets finden, dass die Aufgabe selbst nur entspringt, wo die materiellen Bedingungen ihrer Lösung schon vorhanden oder wenigstens im Prozess ihres Werdens begriffen sind.

XIII. In grossen Umrissen können asiatische, antike, feudale und modern bürgerliche Produktionsweisen als progressive Epochen der ökonomischen Gesellschaftsformation betrachtet werden.

XIV. Die bürgerlichen Produktionsverhältnisse sind die letzte antagonistische, nicht im Sinn von individuellem Antagonismus, sondern eines aus den gesellschaftlichen Lebensbedingungen der Individuen hervorwachsenden Antagonismus, aber die im Schoss der bürgerlichen Gesellschaft sich entwickelnden Produktivkräfte schaffen zugleich die materiellen Bedingungen zur Lösung dieses Antagonismus.

XV. Mit dieser Gesellschaftsformation schliesst daher die Vorgeschichte der menschlichen Gesellschaft ab.

APPENDIX II

"DEMOCRACY AND SOCIALISM",
BY A. ROSENBERG

THE Materialist Conception of History is apt to mar the best historical studies. Professor Arthur Rosenberg's *Democracy and Socialism* (London, 1939) is a well-written and very instructive book. Light is cast on the relations between the Democratic and the Socialist movement ; it is shown how both movements interacted, how for a time they proceeded more or less in common, and then took separate ways. The attitude of Marx and Engels to both movements and their relations to the German Social Democratic Party are set forth. A number of particular phenomena, and some inter-connections that are little known, are brought out, as, for instance, the development and the fate of the Commune in 1871, or the fact that their struggle against anarchism made the German Social Democrats disinclined to serious revolutionary movements.

Though the author abstains from commenting on Marx's theory of history, he shows in every sentence that he believes in it. This attitude does not derogate from the positive qualities of the work. The connection that really exists between economic conditions and political movements is properly revealed ; for instance, the author shows how, in the revolution of 1848, the social and economic structure of society involved the split between the democratic middle class and the labour movement. The situation, however, is not always equally clear and simple. According to the Marxist theory it is, of course, sufficient to confront economic conditions and political development, the latter being regarded without further examination as the

257

consequence of the former. We have shown how rash and un-founded such conclusions generally are. We regret to find that the author is doubtless of the opinion that in such cases the last word is said and all has been explained in a satisfactory way. And in those cases in which the theory proves insufficient to explain an event or a development, Rosenberg, like all Marxists, resorts to words that serve as stop-gaps.

He calls it a " miracle " that the middle-class Republicans could rule France from 1876 to 1879; and that they again obtained the preponderance in the 'nineties was "unnatural"; and quite as "unnatural" was the Liberal Government in England before the Great War. Now, the words " miracle " and " unnatural " express nothing more than that these facts were not in accordance with Marx's theory.

The author likes to give a theoretical form to what is only a record of facts. He says " Liberalism is the constitutional form of early capitalism ", instead of saying that in some countries early capitalism was attended by a Liberal constitu-tion. As such a law does not exist, the author is forced to admit exceptions, though in some cases the exceptions are passed over in silence.

When the author describes different political developments in different countries, he should set forth the reasons for this difference; why, for instance, was Liberalism powerless to overcome the influence of the feudal monarchy in Germany and Austria, as the author states on p. 251 ? The causes would not be found to have been of a purely economic nature. And it is clearly no explanation at all when the author says on p. 276: " The Socialist movement from 1889 to 1914 is the historical result of the development of the European Proletariat. This form of the labour movement and no other was bound to follow from the prerequisites which had formed themselves and existed in 1889." That is true of all movements and all events without exception; they are bound to follow from their pre-requisites or causes; we regret to see the author indulge in such tautologies.

It is true that the author says on p. 275: " The answers to these questions flow naturally from the opinions which had, during the last third of the nineteenth century, gradually developed among Socialist workmen ". Here the author is near the truth. Often he is quite near it without being able to see it. Speaking of the Boulangist movement, he says on p. 247 : " The first general who looked well on horseback, who preached revenge, and who was ill-used by politicians, seemed to the people to embody all their dreams ". He states on p. 297 that " the fundamental error of the German Revisionists was that they did not realise the true character and import of Imperialism ". And again on the same page : " Popular Marxism had lost all its revolutionary fire and all its practical political principles and qualities. But it afforded the Socialist workman a certain pride, a consolation, and a hope for the future almost reminiscent of a religious movement." Or on p. 327 : " After the Great War the popular wing of the Imperialists entered upon a systematic propaganda among the masses, reviling the principles of Democracy, and vied with the Communists in praising Dictatorship ". In several other passages the author thus lays stress on the importance of ideology without ever drawing the necessary deduction from his own insight, though he goes as far as to say on p. 379 : " Liberal Democracy was first manœuvred out of all its positions by ideological methods and was then trodden down by its ruthless opponents ".

Not a few misleading statements are due to the author's preference for abstract expressions, for " isms " and " ologies ", instead of setting men and events before us. He says himself on p. 339 that such abstract formulations are not of much use, and that only the exact investigation of isolated phenomena and events can further our political and historical understanding, yet in his own exposition he seldom goes beyond mere generalisations.

Once, however, he mentions a decisive fact, in describing how the defeat of the Commune was made possible by Bismarck's setting free the French divisions in German captivity and putting them at the disposal of the French Government. The author would probably explain that Bismarck acted in the interest, and as an exponent of, his class. Yet another less resolute and daring statesman would never, in spite of all class interest, have set the prisoners free. The Marxist theory is unwilling to see, in fact incapable of seeing and explaining, the decisive part played by the individual.

That, by his policies and by his successes, Bismarck alone created, in a time of liberal, humanitarian and socialist currents, a reaction of absolutism, as Richelieu alone had done two centuries before him, is a fact which they are unable to grasp. Richelieu established absolutism for more than a century ; how long the reaction inaugurated by Bismarck will last is unknown.

Professor Rosenberg's work is based on a thorough knowledge of his subject and contains very enlightening information on a number of important phenomena. It is the theory whose adherent he is, that causes its shortcomings, and we discussed it in this place for this reason.

INDEX OF NAMES

INDEX